Working on reading

a practical approach to teaching reading

CONTENTS

INTRODUCTION FOR TUTORS

1 WHERE DO YOU START?

2 REVIEWING PROGRESS

3 PLANNING A PROGRAMME

4 BITS AND PIECES

5 RESOURCES FOR PHOTOCOPYING

INTRODUCTION FOR TUTORS

WHO IS IT FOR?

Working on reading is for anyone helping people to develop reading skills. It is for:

★ staff working in Employment Training

★ tutors on adult basic education programmes

★ staff on Youth Training Schemes

★ lecturers in colleges of further education

★ employers and work supervisors

★ those who train and support the tutors

★ anyone else who is teaching reading skills.

It may be most useful if you

★ are new to this type of teaching

★ do not teach reading as part of your main job

★ would like some new ideas.

WHAT IS IT?

It is a guide for practitioners; those who teach reading on a one-to-one or group basis to people who need help in:

★ finding work

★ coping with a course

★ passing an exam

★ changing jobs

★ learning skills for work

★ coping with everyday life.

WHAT IS IN IT?

It is arranged in five sections.

1 Where do you start?

Discusses some issues for those who do not feel confident with reading. It looks briefly at the school system and how it is changing, describes various methods of appropriate initial assessment, and gives a brief introduction to the skill of reading.

2 Reviewing progress

Describes various ways the important process of reviewing can be carried out.

Sections 1 and 2 take you through a series of activities designed to increase awareness of the processes involved in teaching reading. These are optional but will be especially useful if you are new to this type of teaching.

3 Planning a programme

Provides practical support for tutors. It starts with two case studies showing how programmes have been planned. It gives practical help on using the wide range of materials available and gives lots of ideas for teaching reading.

It includes detailed session plans, both for individuals and groups. They are full of ideas that can be adapted for others depending on the situation.

4 Bits and pieces

This is a collection of ideas. It includes:

★ notes on checking reading levels

★ examinations — where they fit in

★ games which may help — published and home-made

★ resources — books, software, video, audio etc

★ sources of help — local and national organisations, resource centres, publishers.

5 Resources for photocopying

The handouts that accompany the assessment section and the practical session plans.

HOW TO USE IT

Section 1 can be worked through as an open learning course, especially if you are new to teaching reading skills or want to rethink your approach. Or it could be used as a reference source of ideas.

OTHER BOOKS IN THE SERIES

Working on reading is accompanied by *Working on writing* and *Working on number.*

They are broadly similar in theme and approach, designed to support tutors in the same practical way.

1 WHERE DO YOU START?

WHAT ARE THE ISSUES?

The fact that you have chosen to read this book indicates that you are probably a confident and competent reader who is helping, or aiming to help, others with their reading.

You need to start thinking about what reading means for you, as well as for those you want to help. For example:

★ why are you reading this book?

★ what do you want to get out of it?

★ who do you want to help with their reading?

★ what and why do they want to read?

★ what do you know already about reading?

★ how do you feel about reading?

★ how do you yourself read?

★ how did you learn to read?

Reading is not simply a matter of learning the ABC. Neither should it be

'... an obscure topic enveloped in a dense fog of pedagogical mystique and mythology'.
(*Essays into literacy,* Frank Smith, Heinemann Educational Books, 1983)

This book aims to help you focus on:

★ what reading is

★ how to assess someone's reading skills

★ how to help them improve those skills.

To begin with, have a look at some facts and figures.

Some research findings

Who are they?

In 1981 over 12,500 British 23-year-olds were asked about their lives as part of a long-term study of people born in the week 3rd to 9th March 1958 (the National Child Development Study).

10% said they had serious problems with reading and writing and a further 4% said they found basic maths extremely difficult. Assuming those people are representative of the community as a whole, the survey meant that about 6 million adults in the UK have literacy and numeracy problems.

One in five in the survey who said they had literacy or numeracy problems admitted that the problems prevented them from

> finding work
>
> finding a better job
>
> getting promotion
>
> doing work-related training or education courses.

Very few (1:10 men and 1:20 women) had attended classes or courses to improve those skills.

4% of the 12,500 people reported problems with reading and most of those also found spelling and writing very difficult. About half of them said this caused everyday difficulties, especially with forms and letters, and many problems connected with work.

In the 1980s the MSC inquired into literacy and numeracy needs of long-term unemployed people and concluded that at least 20% had significant difficulties.

Other countries find much the same evidence — the USA, France and West Germany, all with very different education systems from ours, find significant numbers of adults with literacy and numeracy problems.

Adults reading

The issues considered in this section relate to some of these findings, in particular:

★ attitudes to reading

★ why adults need to read

★ how people cope without being able to read well

★ why some adults do not learn to read well

★ how reading fits in with speaking and writing

★ how a good reader reads.

It also includes some activities. They encourage you to explore the issues more thoroughly by getting you to focus on your own experience and that of people you know.

The skills of reading, and how to help develop them, are covered later.

Attitudes to reading

Activity

Exploring your attitudes to reading

Put your answers in the spaces. Then look at 'Our thoughts' below.

1 How do you rate yourself as a reader? Give yourself a score out of ten.

2 How do you feel about having to read something difficult? Tick the words you think apply or add your own.

anxious   I get butterflies in my stomach   reasonably OK

I look forward to it   basically OK   don't mind at all

I don't particularly care if I can read it or not

I'll do it only if I really have to   a challenge I enjoy

I don't care what people think if I can't do it

3 How would you feel about having to read aloud to colleagues or supervisors? Tick the words you think apply or add your own.

anxious   I get butterflies in my stomach   reasonably OK

I look forward to it   basically OK   don't mind at all

I don't particularly care if I can read it or not

I'll do it only if I really have to   a challenge I enjoy

I don't care what people think if I make a fool of myself

4 What do you think of people who can't read well? Tick the words you think apply or add your own.

stupid   a bit odd   scatter-brained

same as anyone else   maybe had a hard time in life

uninterested   good with hands, though   basically OK

none of these

Put your own words here:

5 If you found out that someone you know couldn't read well, how would you react?

surprise   alarm   shock   try to help   no reaction

horror   anxiety   think it's OK, just different

Any other thoughts of your own?

6 How do you think they might feel?

ashamed   afraid   angry   shy   none of these

Any other thoughts of your own?

Our thoughts

People with reading difficulties often feel ashamed and afraid to admit to them. This is not surprising. If you reacted with horror, surprise or anxiety to the idea that someone you *know* might be 'illiterate', your reaction explains their fear. There is a widespread belief in our society that people *should* have learned to read at school, and that you must be somehow special or odd if you did not.

PEOPLE WHO CANNOT READ ALSO BELIEVE THAT, AND THAT IS WHY THEY OFTEN HIDE THE PROBLEM.

In fact, as 13% of the population report literacy problems, the fact is that it is *normal* to have them. There is nothing to be ashamed of. The assumption that normal people read well is not correct.

'It's like a wig. If you wear one, you don't want people to know you're wearing one. But you take it off at home and you know very well you're bald underneath.' (trainee in Employment Training, 1988)

Being able to read seems to be fundamental to self-respect in this competitive and highly literate society. It makes a big difference to your chances in life, both in developing your own potential and in other people's attitudes to it.

'I hate the words people use to talk about my problem: illiterate, inadequate, ignorant, uneducated, educationally disadvantaged - that's not me!'

Why read?

 **Activity**

Why do you read?

This focuses on the many reasons why adults read.

Jot down all the reading you have done in the last 24 hours; at work, at home and for other reasons. Put them in the spaces and then compare your notes with our thoughts.

At work

At home

Other

Our thoughts

You were probably able to make a long list.

You read for information in newspapers and magazines, labels on containers, to follow instructions, to find your way around, to comment on a report, personal letters, official letters, forms, stories, children's homework, enjoyment...

You may also read lots of different-looking things, for example:

You may use newspapers, television and radio guides, reference books, dictionaries, diaries or calendars, or computers. You may have noted many more.

So there is no shortage of things to read and reasons for reading them.

 **Activity**

How important is reading?

This looks at the importance of reading to *you*.

Jot down some thoughts on these questions:

<u>1</u> Jot down three reasons why is it important for you to read.

1 ....

2 ....

3 ....

<u>2</u> What difference would it make if you could not have read one of the things you read every day? Write down two differences you can think of.

1 ....

2 ....

Our thoughts

From all your answers it has probably emerged that you need to read things to get things done. The range might be from practical matters, like finding the name of a plumber to fix a burst pipe, to relaxation and enjoyment, like reading the paper, a magazine or a good novel. You never read for its own sake; you are always reading *something* for a *reason.*

Reading helps you to do what you want. But if you can't read you have to find other, more complicated ways of achieving the same things.

People need to read more as the amount of print increases year by year. You may remember the days when there were steady, reasonably well-paid jobs which did not involve much reading, writing or maths. But there are fewer of those today. There are more robots around to do many of the repetitive jobs people did; for example, on assembly lines. Yet at the same time computer users need a high level of reading and writing to enter and retrieve data. More jobs these days ask you to think, read and write more and more.

Think also of the reading you often have to do just to get a job.

🏃 Activity

Reading for jobs

Make a note of all the reading you think would be involved in looking for a job.

....
....
....
....
....
....
....
....
....
....
....
....
....

Our thoughts

Reading tasks include:

★ newspaper adverts

★ jobcentre cards

★ employment agency files or cards

★ company information

★ application forms

★ interview letters

★ expenses forms

★ benefit forms

★ official letters

★ contract of employment

★ trades union details

and much more.

This is the aspect which was a problem for the largest number of people in the survey.

Having your say

'People need expertise in language to be able to participate effectively in a democracy.'
(Kingman Report, March 1988)

To do that you have to read — at home, in the family, at work, in the community, on holiday.

Even when you actually cast your vote in elections, you read the ballot card, find the polling station, go in the correct door, find your street on a list on a board, read the names on the ballot paper, read the instructions in the booth, know where to put your ballot paper afterwards. Most of these may be done with other people around, probably from your own neighbourhood, so it might be embarrassing to make mistakes. Would you be tempted to opt out?

How do people manage?

Activity

What's it like when you can't read?

This looks at how you deal with a situation in which you cannot read.

Here are some instructions on using a personal stereo player, in Finnish. Read them to see how to operate it. Then answer the questions and compare notes with our thoughts.

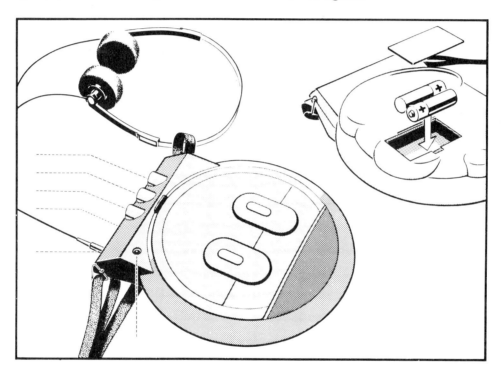

PARISTOT
• Sijoita sinne lokeron ohjeen mukaisesti kaksi alkaliparistoa, koko R6, UM-3 tai AA, ks. kuvaa.
• Paristot ovat kuluneet loppuun, kun ilmaisin BATTERY CHECK syttyy yksiselitteinen toiston aikana (PLAY).
• Poista paristot, kun ne ovat kuluneet tai kun niitä ei tarvita pitkään aikaan.

KASETTIEN TOISTO
• Mikäli haluat, yhdistä stereokuulokkeet liitäntään PHONES ⌂. Sisäänrakennettu kaiutin ei tällöin toimi.
• Avaa kasettilokero ja syötä kasetti vastapäätä painikkeet ja täysi kela oikealla.
• Aloita toisto painamalla PLAY.
• Säädä äänenvoimakkuus VOLUME-säätimellä.
• Pysäytä toisto painamalla STOP.
• Nauhan loputtua PLAY-kytkin vapautuu automaattisesti ja nauhurista katkeaa virta.

PIKAKELAUS
Pikakelaa eteenpäin painamalla F.FWD. PLAY-kytkin vapautuu. Pysäytä pikakelaus painamalla STOP.

HOITO
• Puhdista magneettipäät noin 50 käyttötunnin välein toistamalla puhdistuskasetti, esim. SBC 114, tavallisen kasetin tavoin.
• Älä jätä laitetta tai kasetteja pitkäksi aikaa liian kuumaan paikkaan, esim. lämmityslaitteiden lähelle, auringonpaisteeseen tai aurinkoon pysäköityyn autoon.
• Varo ettei kasetteihin eikä laitteeseen pääse hiekkaa. Älä säilytä kasetteja TV:n tai kaiuttimien lähellä.

Oikeus muutoksiin varataan.

Tyyppinumero on ilmoitettu laitteen takaseinässä, sarjanumero on merkitty paristolokeroon.

13

1 How did you work out what to do?

2 Which words say 'press, cassette, batteries'?

3 How did you find those out?

4 What do you think you may have missed?

Our thoughts

Assuming you are not a fluent Finnish reader already, you may have tackled this task in a variety of ways, eg

★ asked someone who does read Finnish to read out the instructions to you

★ used your prior knowledge of how to operate a personal stereo to look for clues

★ followed the pictures

★ got someone else to do it

★ given up completely

★ said you were too busy to be bothered with it at the moment and hoped someone else would do it

★ felt bewilderment, frustration, anger, embarrassment.

You were in the same position as someone who cannot read. How would you have felt if you had to do this to survive?

Different approaches

It is useful to look at the way people deal with basic skills problems as a question of approach or attitude. Different people behave so very differently; in some cases, the way they feel about the problem and how that affects their behaviour is more important than the actual basic skills. In other cases, the skills themselves are the only things that need to be dealt with.

One tutor said:

'Two students illustrate this rather well. One was very confident in all aspects of life. He had not learned to read as a child. He was a success in his career until the farm he had been running got into trouble. It had never been necessary to read; now it was, so he just decided to learn. He was completely unworried about admitting to it. The reactions he got in places like post offices used to amuse him!

Perhaps the exact opposite was a woman who felt so desperately embarrassed about her not-very-bad spelling problem that she used to get nervous headaches. She was on various voluntary committees; if it was her turn to take minutes of meetings, she always had a headache. She could actually read and write quite well; just felt desperately ashamed of her few odd spelling mistakes.'

Herbert Kohl, in *Reading, how to,* describes four typical ways of reacting to problems:

★ panic

★ evasion

★ coping

★ dealing.

Panic
This is where someone is too frightened to be able to solve the problem; as one (now quite famous) literacy student put it:

'Fear − What Is It?
To me it is someone handing me a form and saying fill this in. Every part of my body stiffens. I go hot and cold all over and there is a little man in my head BASHING MY BRAINS WITH A HAMMER.

Why do people not understand that just because you cannot read and write YOU ARE NOT STUPID?'

People who panic need to learn to manage the panic, and solve the problem where it happens. It is no good learning to fill in a form in private if the panic comes back every time you have to do it in public.

Evasion

This too will need to be addressed as part of the learning programme. This kind of person has adopted the method of avoiding things that are too difficult or challenging, or which threaten to make them feel embarrassed. They will need to learn skills like

★ being able to ask for help (from the right people, in the right way, at the right time)

★ getting equipped with some prompts and supports (lists of difficult words to spell; pre-filled-in cheques etc).

Coping

This is better than panic or evasion. It includes having all the techniques you need to get by, like the ones listed in 'Evasion'. There are others to be identified later.

Dealing

The ideal. This means that you are only interested in solving the problems; you are not worried as well. You just tackle them as needed, and find the best ways to do that.

You know how to ask for help.

You know how to manage the situation if you cannot get help.

You are confident.

How do people fail to learn?

Activity

Why might you fail to learn?

This activity is to help you focus on the reasons for failure to learn.

It may a take little while. Start it straight away and come back to it each time you get a chance to talk to someone.

Ask three people (learners, colleagues, friends or relations) about their memories of learning to read.

Ask each person these questions:

1 How were you taught to read? What are your strongest memories of learning to read?

2 Did you have problems?

First person
1 How taught - strongest memories?

2 Problems?

Second person
1 How taught - strongest memories?

2 Problems?

Third person
1 How taught - strongest memories?

2 Problems?

Our thoughts

Now read these quotes . . .

'It was just simply the teachers had no time for you. You sat in a row and you got to read a book. You get hold of a book. Everyone gets hold of a book. They start from the front. One reads one line. The second pupil reads the second line and so on. And when it gets to you, if you can't read it, he just says, "Right, forget about you. Go over to the next one".'
(*A good life,* Alan, Gatehouse Project, 1977)

'I always found reading slow and hard, and I don't read books for pleasure. At grammar school, in English classes the whole class had to read, say, a chapter of Great Expectations, silently, in the lesson and then answer questions on it. I could never read that fast so I could never finish the work.'

'Reading was always hard work whether I was standing by the teacher and reading to her or trying to keep up if we read round the class. I didn't realise that reading could really be a pleasure until I was 14 or 15.'

It is rare that people over 16 cannot read at all. People can usually read much more than they think – road signs, family names, shop names, words on food packets, television programmes, tools for work and many others.

You will be helping a range of people, from those who can manage no more than a few basic words to those who need more advanced comprehension and speed-reading practice.

Is there a root cause?

There are many reasons why some people do not learn to read confidently. There is no single cause, though there are many common and shared experiences.

'A group of us at school who couldn't read and write very well used to be sent out to do the gardening; it just felt as if they couldn't be bothered. I got further and further behind.'
(carpenter in a basic education evening class)

'I was evacuated to the country from London during the war. I just wasn't really bothered about school after that. Everything else was so much more interesting and exciting that I sort of gave up.'
(trainee in Employment Training)

'I had a trainee in one of my classes who sometimes didn't seem to grasp what was going on. Although he wore glasses, it turned out that the prescription was wrong. What was a reading problem was soon put right once he got new glasses.'
(college lecturer)

Teachers are not to blame for everything, but it is fair to say that schooling is usually geared towards the majority of students who can learn at roughly the same rate as the rest of their age group.

Dyslexia

There are very few people who have such a severe perceptual problem that they cannot learn to read and you are unlikely to meet them. Later sections deal with reading skills that nearly everyone can learn. Even advocates of 'dyslexia' use it to refer mostly to spelling which is a different skill from reading.

From the learners' point of view being known as 'dyslexic' may be their only chance of getting individual help with their literacy skills at school, without being thought stupid.

Some people are more radical. Herbert Kohl, for instance, in *Reading, how to* (Open University Press, 1988) suggests that there is no reading problem, only problem teachers and problem schools; and implies, with a certain dry humour, that if walking and talking were taught at school there would be as many mute cripples as non-readers!

Rigid teaching methods may account for some people's difficulties - a diet of 'phonics' or 'look and say' just may not have suited some learners at a crucial time in their development. But largely it seems that people with basic skills problems were not motivated at school.

19

'Children learn to read by reading and the sensible teacher makes reading easy and interesting, not difficult and boring ... the more difficulty children experience in learning to read, the less reading and more nonsense drills we typically arrange for them to do.'
Essays into literacy, Frank Smith, Heinemann Educational Books, 1983)

'I - am - in - the - slow -
read - ers - group - my - broth
er - is - in - the - foot
ball - team - my - sis - ter
is - a - ser - ver - my
litt - le - broth - er - was
a - wise - man - in - the
in - fants - christ - mas - play
I - am - in - the - slow
read - ers - group - that - is
all - I - am - in - I
hate - it.'

('Slow reader', from *Please Mrs Butler,* Allan Ahlberg, Puffin Books, 1984)

Reading, speaking, writing

 Activity

This activity looks at some of the possible areas of confusion.

Consider these statements and use the spaces below to record your thoughts and opinions.

'People can't learn to read if they don't speak English properly.'

'You can't teach people to read by using dialect or wrong grammar.'

'People could learn to spell better if only they would read more.'

Our thoughts

Speaking and listening, writing and reading, are all inextricably linked as communication skills. They are all ways of using language to communicate what people are thinking.

But they are all distinct skills – speaking is a very different activity from listening, and writing is very different from reading. And older learners, even if their reading and writing are at a beginning level, are not beginner speakers or listeners. They know what they want to say and can work out what you want to say to them, or can ask you to explain.

'A beginning reader is not a beginning thinker.'
(*Opening time,* Gatehouse Project, 1985)

Standard English

Most of the written English people need to read is in the standard form, especially at work. Much of it is in the form of brief instructions, abbreviations, and specialised words or phrases. Actually a lot of it is written in 'officialese' which demands its own translation into everyday language. And, as the Kingman Committee found:

'Its edge is sometimes blunted in places of work ... [with] letters or reports expressed in English that is sometimes incomprehensible, or instructions where misuse of words and emphasis creates misunderstanding.'

But adults are quite aware that what is written is not how they or others speak. Reading is primarily about reading for meaning, not about analysing differences in dialect.

Writing involves us in thinking about how we say things, but we usually read things in the understanding that they are written in an agreed code for communication. The fact that people speak different forms of English does not mean they will have problems reading.

Reading and writing

When it comes to words and thoughts in print, reading is easier than writing. Reading involves finding the meaning from print or handwriting that someone else has already put there. So you usually have a head start; you know

★ it will mean something you want to know

★ the words are there on paper for you to consider in your own time, to check in a dictionary for meaning

★ the punctuation and layout have already been decided for you.

A useful technique is for the tutor to write down the learner's words in the exact way they speak them. When they read it back there are two ways it improves their reading skills. First, it uses their own language – the 'grammar' is consistent and appropriate, even though it may not be the same as yours. Second, it means they are reading something meaningful to them – and may be much more interesting than stilted but so-called 'easy' versions of, say, children's stories or 'simplified' adult stories. Writing can help with reading.

But reading cannot help with writing. If your spelling needs improving, reading a lot does not do any good. The skills involved are very different. You don't learn to write by reading. You only learn to write by writing.

Reading intelligently

 Activity

Some knowledge and skills you need

Read this and fill the gaps:
We are a small .... friendly company making .... exciting
range .... hi-tech products. We have .... full order book ....
so have .... number .... vacancies .... our production
department .... we .... looking .... electronic and light
electro-mechanical assemblers. Some basic assembly skills
would .... desirable, but .... you are used .... following
patterns .... making models .... can train you .... this
interesting work. Our basic working week .... 8.30 am 4.30
pm Monday .... Friday .... half .... hour .... lunch.

Now answer these questions and compare your notes with our
thoughts.

1 How did you know what the missing words were?

2 Did the gaps prevent you understanding the meaning?

Our thoughts

You probably found that quite easy. You will have relied heavily
on the words that give the passage its meaning filling in the other
words from your knowledge of how words link together. But they
didn't need to be on the page for you to read them. In this book
these words are called 'structure words'. They are covered later.

Among other things, you demonstrated

★ how to make good guesses from the meaning and context

★ knowledge of how grammar works by linking words together
   logically

★ abilty to interpret full stops.

 **Activity**

Some more skills and knowledge you need

Read this passage and put words into the gaps.

Personnel . . . . can be employed in any . . . . of
organisation. They are to be . . . . in industry, ...
local and central . . . . nationalised . . . . and the
NHS. There are companies who do not treat . . . .
management as a specialisation and who . . . . their
departmental managers and . . . . to deal with all
personnel . . . .

Now answer these questions:

1 Choose three words that you put in the gaps and write down
   how you made your decisions.

	word	how you made your decision
first word		
second word		
third word		

Our thoughts

That was probably more difficult than in the last activity. This
time the words that hold the meaning were left out. In this task
we call these the *meaning carriers*. But it's quite likely that the
words you put in were either the same as in the original text or at
least meant the same . . . or very nearly.

To do this activity you needed to know:

★ something about the subject − if you knew nothing about
   personnel management you will probably have found it hard

★ where to start reading on the page and that the words go from
   left to right and the lines from top to bottom

★ enough other words in the passage to allow you to guess the
   missing ones

★ the function of full stops and commas − knowing that they
   give you permission to pause will have helped you understand it

★ the grammar of English – not the words like noun, verb etc but the way the language is spoken.

The main skill you will have used is guessing or prediction using all the knowledge you already have. You are likely to have read and re-read some parts looking for clues where you could find them. But you will have found it easier if you weren't nervous about it and if you wanted to find out what the missing words were. In other words, if you had the right attitudes.

 # Activity

Now read this text:

'**Myoclonus . . . is rare, occurring occasionally in encephalomyelitis or encephalopathy; sporadically, involving the soft palate, pharynx, diaphragm and sometimes other muscles; or as the rare paramyoclonus multiplex. There is pathological evidence associating non-epileptic myoclonus with disorders of the olivodentate system.**

5 hydroxytryptophan improves some cases of myoclonus and the 5 hydroxytryptophan antagonist methysergide causes a deterioration, suggesting that the brain mechanisms responsible for myoclonus can be inhibited by increasing brain 5 hydroxytryptophan or catecholamines. The benefit is most obvious in post-anoxic myoclonus.'
(*Brain's clinical neurology,* revised by Roger Bannister, OUP, 1978, 5th edition)

Now answer these questions:

1 How did you feel about reading this?

2 Did you read it in a different way from either of the pieces in the previous activity?

3 If the answer to question 2 was 'yes' can you describe how your approach was different?

25

4 Did you understand it? In a couple of sentences could you explain what the passage is about, or what you think it is about?

5 If you did not really understand it, how did you work out what you thought it meant?

6 Write down the words which you have not read before? How did you deal with them?

the word	your method of dealing with it

Our thoughts

That was probably difficult. The reading skills you used for the first passage were still in play for this one. But you may have added:

★ determination to read it

★ looking for familiar words

★ deciding some difficult words, or the whole lot, weren't worth puzzling over – accepting that you don't understand

★ reading and re-reading some parts word for word to get the meaning

★ reading ahead to look for clues

★ sounding out some unfamiliar words letter by letter

★ using your knowledge of where the stress lies in long English words

★ recognising the 'root' part of scientific words

★ breaking words up into manageable chunks

★ looking at the shape, letter sequence and letter patterns of a word, remembering those, then looking it up in a dictionary

★ asking someone who knows the jargon to translate.

But if you're not a medical person the chances are that the meaning of the passage is lost on you – in other words if you knew nothing about the subject before you started reading words you don't understand will not have made you any the wiser.

YOU HAVE TO BE ABLE TO UNDERSTAND THE MEANING OF WHAT YOU READ BEFORE YOU READ IT, IN ORDER TO UNDERSTAND IT WHEN YOU READ IT.

By the way, myoclonus is a 'shock-like muscular contraction', an involuntary jerk or twitch in various parts of the body. It is most common in epilepsy, but can also be the kind of twitch you have when you are falling asleep.

Conclusions

If you think of yourself as a fluent reader, you do all the things described in these three activities without necessarily thinking about them.

Above all, you have the *confidence* to use them all, and to say to yourself 'I don't understand this — it is difficult but I am not stupid' if the going is hard.

The people who need help with reading lack those things. It is virtually certain that they can learn them and that with help, determination and time, they will.

The rest of *Working on reading* looks at how to set about it.

ASSESSING LEARNING NEEDS

There is a wide range of attitudes and skills connected with reading. As the issues are wide ranging, sensitive assessment is a vital part of any programme of help with reading.

Accepting help

It may not always be clear who has problems or what the problems are. People may openly ask for help so it is fairly straightforward to find out their needs. They may see themselves as having 'a problem with spelling' as a term which takes in both writing and reading.

Generally speaking, people who find reading very difficult will also find writing very hard. But poor spellers may be very good readers. Of course, everyone is an individual so generalisations are unsatisfactory. But the tutors need to be aware of the connections between reading and writing.

People may be very painfully aware of the problem, especially if they have failed to get jobs or have lost a job because of it. Some may be aware they have a problem, but refuse to admit it to anyone, and resist offers of help.

Others may hide an inability to cope with the literacy demands of a job by always avoiding situations which require any reading at all.

Some may be making mistakes in their work which neither they nor their immediate supervisor may recognise as a reading problem. They may appear to others to be careless, clumsy, or even dishonest.

'One of our retail trainees had a lot of problems at work with his immediate supervisor — he was always rushing into jobs and his supervisor complained about his hasty "don't care" attitude. He was always doing things wrong. The reality was that he felt so nervous about reading that he ignored it altogether and just went ahead and did what he hoped was right.'
(YTS tutor)

The tutor's role

As a tutor, you seek to:

★ establish with someone that there is a reading problem and identify what it is

★ help them get the problem into perspective, to reassure them that they are not a failure or a freak

★ find out the most appropriate strategies for that person to improve their reading skills

★ work out together a programme of helpful practice in those strategies and skills

★ help them recognise their own strengths and develop their confidence.

The starting point

This section gives some ideas about how to assess needs and decide a starting point for your programme.

 **Activity**

Your scheme picture

This activity may take some time and you may not be able to start it straight away. You might need to talk to someone else where you work, possibly your manager, to help you get a complete scheme picture.

Before you look at the various ways of assessing learners' needs, it is worth starting by looking at the methods you are using now — your present 'scheme picture'.

1 Put down brief details of how you assess prospective learners' reading skills at present.

2 What materials do you use?

3 What reading skills do you think are needed by the people you work with?

4 How do you think people like to be helped?

Our thoughts

There are several ways of assessing learners. Different methods work for different people and different situations. But when you have looked through the next section you may decide that some approaches might suit you, your environment and your learners.

ASSESSMENT TECHNIQUES

As the tutor, you may:

★ look

★ ask and listen

★ use a checklist

★ make an individual profile

★ use a test

★ combine more than one approach.

Look

The first stage is to be an observer. In some situations any kind of formal assessment is impossible, but if you want to help learners improve their reading you may look out for those who:

★ ask for help with forms

★ avoid reading anything, perhaps saying that they know it already or will read it later

★ always stay very quiet when others are answering questions on something they have read

★ often appear to have got completely the wrong end of the stick from a training session, from instructions or notes from other people

★ say they haven't got their glasses with them

★ get very defensive about not having followed written instructions

★ avoid writing anything

★ are often off sick at times when a lot of reading and writing are required.

Advantages

1 You can do this kind of observation informally at any time while getting on with other things.

2 It can become an established part of normal routine.

Risks

1 If people think you are watching them in this way they may feel uneasy and react defensively.

2 You must record what you observe, or you risk forgetting or misremembering important clues.

'I always say I'm in a hurry, and say I'll have to take the form home and send it back to the office later. Then my son helps me with it in the evening.'

'I'm a company director and I'm supposed to be really competent reading things. Every day journals come to the company and they get circulated round the directors and senior managers. When they get to me they stop circulating. And it's not because I'm too busy. I just put off starting to read them because I think I'll be too slow. I've always been like this. I had stomach aches at school on library day.'

Ask and listen

This should be an early part of any assessment. Asking and listening skilfully takes some tact and patience.

Advantages

1 People may speak freely about the reasons behind a reading problem, when they meet you, the tutor, who accepts them uncritically.

2 In a group of like-minded people, it may be a relief to share experiences of reading problems.

3 Other problems may emerge — with writing, talking or number skills.

Risks

1 People may feel too vulnerable, especially with a reading problem, to reveal weaknesses publicly.

2 They won't necessarily be able to describe the problem.

3 You may not have enough time to talk in an open-ended way.

4 If you spend too much time with some people, others in the group may resent it.

5 You may not be seen as neutral - that may affect what people are prepared to say.

6 It is difficult to avoid bringing your own attitudes or prejudices about reading, writing and intelligence to this contact.

A tutor's comment:

'I always start by asking what they're doing now and what they would like to do; what kind of job and what kind of skills they think they will need. That is much better than asking what people can't do - once they're talking about what they'd like to do any problems emerge anyway. If people are asking for help with something specific, then both you and they can get a realistic idea of where to start and what you can achieve.'

Use a checklist

This approach is often called 'self-assessment', intended for use by the learner alone. In practice, it is usually much more helpful if the tutor and learner go through this together. It can involve:

★ filling in a form

★ ticking boxes

★ writing answers

★ responding to a computer program

★ looking at selections of print or handwritten texts

★ selecting from a list of 'can do' cards.

It is worth bearing in mind that you are unlikely to be helping the learner with just reading; it is very likely you will be working on writing as well.

So a checklist will need to take account of the links between the various language skills — speaking, listening, reading and writing.

Advantages

1 It can be devised to suit your particular course/purposes/ trainees.

2 It can be thorough and systematic.

3 It can be stopped or dipped into at any time that suits the learner or tutor.

Risks

1 It may suit you rather than the learner.

2 A checklist devised for a different scheme from yours may not cover the reading needed by your learners.

3 It can be very heavy going if the list is too comprehensive.

One example of this approach is in Baselines (ALBSU, 1987). This material comprises a printed pack with a self-assessment computer program. It asks learners how they feel about the kind of reading on the page (forms, letters, food tins, instructions etc) and where they would like help. They enter their responses into the computer, which then gives feedback.

You may like to use a checklist in table form. One example is the checklist 'How's your reading?' in Section 5, 'Resources for photocopying', which can be photocopied or adapted to suit your programme.

Make an individual profile

Like checklists, profiles can be very easily used for assessment or review at any stage.

You and/or the learner record all the reading they do or need in their work or everyday life. You then note the knowledge and skills that are involved, so that you can decide what the problems are and where to begin.

Advantages

1 An individual profile is 'learner-centred', ie designed to match the needs of individuals very closely.

2 People can say what bothers them most; their priorities become the list.

3 Even if you only have a few minutes together, or if someone is too nervous to speak much, you are able to make a start, taking their lead.

Risks
1 To use this profile for continuous review, you have to be very organised.

2 You have to be an experienced analyst of the problems.

3 It can take a long time to work out.

An example:

Name:	Date:
Purpose for reading	

There is a blank 'Personal profile' sheet in Section 5, 'Resources for photocopying'.

Use a test

Reading is a fundamental part of entry or aptitude tests set by many employers. Many courses also have tests at intervals. Some require a lot of writing or calculations, others may be multiple-choice question papers. Whatever form they take, they usually involve reading. Problems for learners range from not being able to read more than a few words on the paper to misinterpreting some of the questions set.

Any of those people may be otherwise well suited to a particular job; they probably have many other skills to offer. And just because they can't read the question does not necessarily mean they will not be able to do the job. The reading required lets them down, but it may be letting the employer down as well − the test may have no direct relevance to the workplace.

Since tests are widely used, tutors need to be aware of them. Applicants need to do them under stressful conditions and usually within a strict time limit. It is important to look at the relevance of the test to particular learners. Any that are obviously designed for children, or which involve setting 'reading ages' should be avoided.

Advantages

1 Doing a particular test may be someone's immediate goal. If you have a very short time to help them, reviewing through it with the learner may reveal what aspects of reading they want to work on.

2 A test simulates the pressure under which people actually have to read things at work.

3 Some people like tests.

4 People may be highly motivated by tests which are directly relevant to them.

Risks

1 Failure breeds failure. Because reading is so crucial to other basic skills, a failed reading test may convince learners that they will be no good at anything else either.

2 Unless it is very carefully designed, the test may not reveal particular problem areas.

3 Some published tests have no direct relevance to the workplace.

4 Some tests need to be administered by trained psychologists.

37

You may already have some tests that you give new trainees or learners. It may be worth considering them in the light of the 'risks' above.

Making your own check

In an ALBSU newsletter (May 1988) Judy Vaughan reported on her work on 'Assessing reading in an FE college'. She used the 'cloze' procedure, (the activity you did in the section 'How do good readers read?') and applied it to the exam papers and reading material used on college courses.

There are advantages and risks in that approach. Its main advantage is that you, the tutor, can use the material that is actually used, on the course or in the work routine, to give you a fairly accurate view of the learner's competence in reading. It also means that you can analyse the reading material and decide how appropriate it is for the people who will be using it at work or on a course.

The ALBSU newsletter gives details of how the tests were devised. There is more on the formulas for working out readability in 'Checking reading levels' in Section 4, 'Bits and pieces'.

An example of a text used is:

Finding a builder

The names of local builders can be found in telephone directories and local newspapers. Not all builders are willing to work on relatively _____ jobs such as knocking two rooms into one: some even consider extensions too small.

The best way to _____ a reliable builder is by personal recommendation from someone _____ has recently employed the builder. Then you can find out _____ well the builder cleared up . . .

Combine more than one approach

All these approaches can be combined in any way you choose. As initial assessment tools they may not give you all the answers. If they are used or adapted for continuous reviewing of progress, they can be extremely valuable.

Assessment in practice

 **Activity**

Case studies

Read these. In each case decide

★ which assessment method(s) you think are most suitable

★ what you would do

★ how you might follow through this first assessment during the course.

Case study 1

An Employment Training manager is running a variety of training programmes, eg bricklaying, car mechanics, word processing, gardening, painting and decorating. The managers and supervisors are aware that some trainees have difficulty with reading, writing and maths.

What would you advise them to do?

Case study 2

Alan started on a Youth Training Scheme wanting to do retail work. He began to put himself down from his first contact with the scheme staff, both in relation to his literacy and to his social acceptability. He would say 'I can't read and write' and 'I'm no good at anything'. He seemed to be making himself out to be incompetent and unacceptable to the group.

What would you do?

Case study 3

Three sisters, one 17, one 19 and one 23, from a traveller family asked at an adult education centre for help with reading and writing. They had never been to school but now wanted to learn. The youngest sister wanted to take her driving test. The oldest sister was applying for a council house. The other sister wanted to help her younger brothers with reading.

What would you advise the tutor to do?

What they did

You might be interested to know what did happen in each of these cases.

Case study 1

The manager set up some training sessions for supervisors to help them identify literacy and numeracy needs. He also asked a specialist tutor to assess and teach any trainees who needed this help. The tutor talked with each trainee for 45 minutes and drew up a profile with them of their needs.

Case study 2

The tutor put together a checklist of basic reading and writing skills that would be required at work. She realised that his attitude was due to a lack of confidence in himself. The checklist provided a list of things that in fact he could do, so they then set priorities from the other tasks that had been chosen for the list.

Case study 3

The adult basic education tutor talked with the sisters for about ten minutes on their first meeting as part of the normal evening class routine. They would all be leaving the area in three months' time when the fruit-picking season started and then returning after the summer. On their first meeting, the sisters and the group tutor were on unfamiliar ground, so the tutor decided to have a detailed discussion/assessment later in the term. This took place after five weeks and took the form of a profile for each person.

THE SKILLS OF READING

A cautionary tale. . .

In the cautionary *Tale of Thomas Mead,* Thomas finds himself in prison because he refused to read public signs.

In the end, his fellow prisoners, not his school teachers, succeeded in helping him, because they had a clearer view of what reading is for:

His cellmates thought it was a crime
that Thomas Mead was doing time,
and all because he couldn't read.
'Please help me to!' cried Thomas Mead.

They taught him words he ought to know,
like UP and DOWN and STOP and GO,
IN and OUT, EMPTY, FULL,
EXIT, ENTRANCE, PUSH and PULL,
and WASHROOM, LADIES, GENTLEMEN,
and DANGER, WET PAINT, WALK, DON'T RUN,
and then they said they'd better get
him started on the alphabet.

This is a cautionary tale for tutors. The alphabet is not the place to start. You start with the learner's immediate needs.

The aim of the tutor

You do this by taking the mystery out of reading, by making the skills of reading explicit to the learner and sharing knowledge with them on equal terms. It may be the first time that these skills have been explained. And tutors often find that they learn more about reading by doing the explaining.

'It is important for people who care to help others learn to read to have patience and understand that the crucial thing for learners is to learn as much as possible how to teach themselves.'
(Reading, how to, Herbert Kohl, Open University Press, 1988)

To teach reading it helps to have a strategy; a plan. There are three main parts to this plan.

The first part ...

Learners need to

★ feel confident to have a go

★ have a purpose for reading; knowing what they want to read and why

★ feel at ease at the level they choose.

The second part . . .

Learners need to know what the skills of reading are – these need to be explained and shared.

And finally . . .

Learners need to be able to know how, when and where to use these skills.

The different parts of this plan are:

★ attitudes; confidence, purpose, feeling at ease

★ knowledge

★ use of reading skills.

These are described briefly below, together with a note about levels of reading and useful approaches and aids to teaching.

Attitudes

Confidence

What learners need most is confidence, just as anyone who is learning anything needs it. People whose reading gives them difficulties are probably lacking in confidence much more than most.

A confident reader can

★ read familiar texts

★ try new and complex words

★ make mistakes and learn from them

★ stop when they've had enough.

Purpose

Everyone has their own purposes for reading. These may coincide, especially where people have to work together and need to read the same things. But they may be highly individual.

Feeling at ease

Confidence has a lot to do with this. The tutor needs to find out what the main stress on the learner is when it comes to reading. It may be a fear of reading aloud, anxiety about computer screens or a feeling of having to read the whole course textbook in one go.

Both tutors and learners can learn to relax with reading.

Knowledge

The aim is to give them as many clues as possible to help them extract the meaning from the page and to give them confidence to know when and how to use this knowledge.

Words go from left to right; lines from top to bottom

This may seem very basic but it is important especially for people whose first language was written right to left (like Urdu) and top to bottom (like Japanese). The only reason for English being presented on the page the way it is is cultural and it has to be learnt. This is not saying that our eyes only move from left to right and from top to bottom when we read (see the next section on 'Use of reading skills').

Structure words

These are so called because they provide a framework for the words that carry the meaning. A list of these is given in Section 5, 'Resources for photocopying'. One hundred of them make up half of all the reading material learners will ever meet. Knowing this can be a comfort!

Social words

Some of these are shown in Section 5, 'Resources for photocopying'. They are words on public signs in common use, words in shop windows etc. Many beginning readers know many more of these than they think at first. The main thing about them is that they are always seen in context, so people know that the car with POLICE on the side usually has police officers inside, not chimpanzees. Reading does not have to be all plain-clothes work.

Letter names and the alphabet sequence

Letter names ('ay, bee, cee' etc) may seem too basic. But sometimes beginning readers are unsure of some letters. Knowing the sequence of the alphabet is important when you use indexes, directories and lists etc. It may be that some learners are not sure of the sequence, so do not take it for granted.

The shape of letters and words

This includes the way letters are formed, the differences between capital and lower case letters, different styles of print and other people's handwriting, and the shape of words that helps people recognise them. As a tutor you are helping learners recognise the significant features of words. Maybe their length or a particular letter is the clue they are looking for.

Letter sounds and patterns

Learners need to know that there is no one-to-one correspondence between the letters and the sounds they make. The position of a letter within a word and the way it combines with other letters changes its sound. People may be familiar with these as 'spelling rules' or 'word families'.

Syllables, parts of words and emphasis

Knowing that words break into manageable bits is useful at all levels as you may have found for yourself in an earlier activity with a word like 'encephalomyelitis'. You may have looked for parts of the word and possibly recognised how to say it by knowing where the emphasis came.

Grammar

People use grammar in their speech all the time, without having to know the jargon. It is helpful for the learner to keep talk about grammar to the minimum. The important thing is that if someone can talk they have an adequate command of grammar to help in reading. It does not matter it there are slight differences between the 'grammar' of the reader and the 'grammar' of the piece being read. Most people are sufficiently aware of other grammatical constructions and there are plenty of other clues to help.

Punctuation and layout

Again beware of too much here. Punctuation often makes a difference to the meaning of a text, and layout is important for readability and meaning. The reader needs to know that sometimes the clues they are looking for are very small.

Use of reading skills

If learners are in control, they will be able to choose the appropriate skill(s) to suit the reading task. The important message is to choose what seems to work and to try a different approach if the first or second one doesn't work.

Predicting — getting meaning and purpose from the context

It is useful to know that you can use all the clues available – whether they come from the pictures, the reader's knowledge of the subject, the words that have gone before, the words that are still to come, the title of the chapter or anything else. Readers need to know that it is OK to 'predict' backwards by reading on as well as forwards. Many less confident readers do not dare 'guess' words for fear of getting them wrong. More confident readers do it all the time. The tutor can make the fear worse by insisting on every word being exactly as it is on the page.

Reading between the lines

Many official letters or forms almost demand you read between the lines for meaning. Newspaper reports certainly do. Readers at all levels can be encouraged to trust their own judgment on what something means. This is a development of the skill of prediction; reading what is implied as well as what is actually written down.

Skimming and scanning

These skills can be used at all levels, though perhaps more as the learner speeds up. They are vital for study skills.

Using a dictionary and reference material

Learners at all levels may be unsure about these. It may be because they are not sure of the alphabet, or have never used a filing system before, or do not dare touch a computer.

Proofreading

This is a reading skill but It has more to do with writing than reading. It is an essential for checking your own or other people's writing.

Asking for help

The skill here is knowing who to ask and how. To know who is appropriate and to be able to ask in a way that doesn't make the reader feel humiliated.

Choosing what they want to read

This means asking in the library if the leaflets on housing benefit on display are the latest ones or in a bookshop if anything else is available on the subject of growing onions. It means looking at different presentations of the same material of, for example DIY books and deciding the best one for the purpose.

2 REVIEWING PROGRESS

WHY REVIEW?

 Activity

Before you start reading this section, briefly answer these questions. The idea is just to start thinking about the reviewing process.

1 Why review?

2 Who should do it?

3 What is being reviewed?

4 How often?

5 Where?

6 What if you and the learner disagree?

7 What forms can the review take?

Our thoughts

Reviewing is an essential process. It is important to everyone to know how they're doing at regular intervals, not just at the end of a course. It is also important for the tutor to know whether their approaches are successful. This can only happen if records are made and kept of what has been achieved and how the learner feels about it. It should always be a two-way process; learner and tutor together can then plan future learning or report to an employer or supervisor.

There is no perfect way to review; as with the first assessment, you will need to take into account the needs of the learners and the constraints on you as a tutor.

From the previous section you may have decided which form or forms of initial assessment will suit you and your learners. You might choose to use or adapt that system to review progress.

What you choose to do depends on

★ your own situation

★ the time you have available

47

★ the frequency of your contact

★ the numbers of people involved.

REVIEWING IDEAS

Involving the learner

The important thing is to involve the learner in the review process, whichever form it takes. Neither you nor they may be used to this, but there are many ways to approach it. It is essential for the learner to succeed. They will only want to go on if someone feels the learning is relevant to them and that they are making progress.

Using initial assessment

This is a useful starting point for the review, since you will have recorded the learners' comments, responses and feelings. The same method can be used or adapted to review progress at appropriate intervals.

Asking and listening

This will usually happen at every meeting, so you will be continually looking and listening for progress.

Checklist

Copies of the same list can be used as when you first met the learner; dated at intervals so that both you and the learner can see how their confidence has developed.

Profile

You could take the one you first drew up, take a few items and chart progress.

Test

This could be used at intervals, but usually only if you are working on a tight schedule up to an entry test or exam.

A review sheet

You could ask the learner to write answers to or talk about questions like:

what work have you done this term/session?

what can you do now that you couldn't do before?

what do you still have problems with?

what do you want to work on next?

how do you feel about the way things are going?

SETTING TARGETS

Regular reviewing can show learners what skills they are mastering, how they feel about them, and what has been successful or unsuccessful. If it is centred on the individual, there is no need to compare learners against each other. What is important is that they are progressing against their own goals.

Setting targets can be a part of every review session. Learners will be better motivated if targets

★ are chosen by them

★ are achievable within a fairly short time, but

★ provide an element of challenge

★ can be measured

★ provide their own reward — maybe a sense of satisfaction and/or approval from someone else.

How to set targets

You might find it useful to take parts of the checklist or profile and make those into explicit targets, with dates and resources noted beside them.

Here is an example of some action plans in which learners set their own reading targets, together with their comments about them.

TARGETS	STEPS	TARGET DATE
(TIM, GARDENER) GARDENING WORDS	GET CATALOGUES	OVER A YEAR
	NOT STUTTERING WHEN READING TO OTHERS	PRACTISE IN CLASS
	HYMNS AT CHURCH	BREAK UP WORDS
(DAVE, PAINT SPRAYER) DIY INSTRUCTIONS	READ IN CLASS AND BY NEXT MONTH	
	JAMES BOND BOOK	
	AT HOME, GET FASTER AT PICKING OUT IMPORTANT WORDS	BY THE SUMMER
(MICHAEL, DRIVER) SPELLING AND READING	BREAK UP WORDS	MAY NOT HAVE MUCH TIME OVER THE NEXT FEW MONTHS
	DICTIONARY WORK	
	FILLING FORMS	

These are all individual targets, which are fairly long term. You may need to help the learner set a series of short-term targets to suit the time available.

You may also be setting targets for a small or large group who may need to be working on the same kind of reading skills as each other. The principles above are just as relevant.

3 PLANNING A PROGRAMME

Before you begin to plan a programme of help, you will have

★ assessed the learners' needs

★ set targets

★ set up a way of recording progress.

All these will have been done in a way designed to build the learners' confidence. They will give you clear aims so that you can plan a programme that is relevant to them.

PLANNING AHEAD

Many factors affect how you plan a learning programme.

Read the list below and decide which affect you. As you read consider what has been left out that might affect you:

★ the time available for teaching, eg for a session, a course, learners on varying contracts

★ the number of people you are teaching; one-to-one or groups

★ how many tutors are involved; how many are specialists in teaching reading, and what training is available

★ learners' short- and long-term goals, eg an entry exam in two weeks, a vocational course next year, open ended

★ needs that emerged from the assessment; skills the learners need to develop

★ what access you and the learners have to resources, especially connected with present or desired work

★ other basic skills learners want to improve, eg writing and numeracy.

 **Activity**

Planning

This asks you to focus on the issues facing you when planning.

Make a list of what affects you when planning a programme.

★ _____

★ _____

★ _____

★ _____

★ _____

★ _____

★ _____

★ _____

Now think about what you have written.

Would you like to make any changes to these circumstances? If the answer is 'yes', use these spaces to write down

★ what it is possible to change

★ when this could happen

★ who else is involved

★ your role in effecting the change

Our thoughts

For a programme to be effective, all these factors must be taken into account. Maybe some could be changed either in the short- or long-term and you could set yourself objectives for carrying out that change.

Released from punishment, to be set free.

Being able to write and also read. The most essential part was being pushed, by a person who really understood.

I'm grateful for all the help you gave. And grateful for pushing me through. I didn't think I could do it. But I did, with help from you.

I'm not prepared to read to others. I'm not prepared to be good. But I am prepared to only change a little bit if I could.

(Staying on; going further, Erica Cook, ABE learner, 1987)

Becoming a better reader

As you start to think about how you are going to help people become better readers, bear in mind that you want to offer help with

★ attitudes − confidence, purpose, feeling at ease

★ knowledge

★ use of reading skills.

PRACTICAL STEPS

This section continues with the practical steps for planning a programme. It offers

★ a 'template' for planning a programme

★ suggestions on finding, adapting and using resources

★ a 'template' for planning individual sessions.

A 'template' approach

One basic principle underpins the kind of teaching or help you are planning: you should follow the learner's lead. This principle has been behind all the assessment and reviewing approaches you have been considering.

These are the essential parts of the template:

★ following the learner's lead

★ appropriate assessment

★ agreeing with the learner:
   the main problem areas
   where to start
   how to proceed
   the best way to work (alone, as a pair, in a group)
   targets (skills, certificates, exams)
   timescale
   who else is involved (supervisors, managers, examiners)
   resources

★ starting from what the learner can do already

★ finding, making or adapting relevant teaching material

★ being prepared to change direction with the learner as needs emerge

★ reviewing progress together, regularly.

The template in action

Case study 1 – Vincent, aged 22, (a trainee on Employment Training working as a cleaner and handyman at an aircraft museum – beginning reader).

★ an appropriate assessment

Vincent was identified as having severe difficulties with reading and other basic skills. He was exceptionally nervous with most people, so on his first meeting with the tutor it was a major achievement that he arrived, stayed and talked for 15 minutes. Given those limitations, the tutor was able to note only that he could write his own name and address and read just a few social words (on cards).

★ the main problem area

For Vincent this was his ability to get on with other people. His self-confidence and self-esteem were very low. He felt he could read a little, but did not dare try. To start with, he would have to be taught in a group of five, all beginning readers. His purpose was to read the details of the aircraft he was working around. He loved the job at the museum.

★ where to start

It was agreed to start with reading social words and signs around people at work.

★ how to proceed

They would find out what signs Vincent and the rest of the small group needed to know.

★ the targets

1 to increase Vincent's confidence to tackle reading, writing and maths (long term)
2 to persuade members of the group to join an adult basic education evening class (long term)
3 to read some short adult basic reader stories (short term).

★ the timescale

Trainees came on the programme at any time in the year. This course of 20 sessions (each 90 minutes long) would lie in the middle of Vincent's 12 months on the programme. But the small group would change during that period because of the variations in other people's contracts.

★ who else was involved

Transport was arranged for some trainees to come to the programme centre for tuition once a week. This involved supervisors as well as office staff to arrange things.

★ resources

The tutor was able to use any of the programme's paperwork (forms, leaflets, contracts etc). Some money was budgeted to buy a small number of adult literacy and numeracy books. A small room, with table and chairs was available each time. Paper, files, pens, pencils and notebooks were provided for the trainees.
A flipchart, video recorder and photocopier were available.

★ the best way to work

There was time enough only to work in a small group once a week for 90 minutes. In group activities, other members could work in pairs and help each other. Vincent needed the support of the tutor at all times. He often arrived earlier than the others, so 15 minutes' individual attention prepared him for the stress of taking part in the group.

What actually happened

★ start from what the learner can do already

They started with familiar social words on cards and talking about where these would be seen. Vincent was pleased and surprised that he knew more than some of the other members of the group. He was also able to read and write the day's date, days of the week, months of the year and his own address with more success than some of the others. This made it easier for him to practise those words on forms in front of the others.

★ find, make or adapt teaching material

For Vincent these were, eg, the aircraft museum leaflet, a letter written by him to another museum and an airship manufacturer to ask for information, their replies, timesheet and application form, ABE published worksheets and stories, his own writing, letter dominoes.

★ be prepared to change direction

After a number of sessions, Vincent decided on a further target; to do 'joined-up writing'. Working on this gave him extra confidence in his ability to write and the impression others had of him.

★ monitor progress regularly

At every session they talked about progress made. At the end of 10 and 20 sessions, each member completed an evaluation form with the tutor saying how they felt — what they could do better than before, what they would like to work on next, what were the problems etc. Three copies of the form were made — one for the trainee, one for the programme manager to act as a report, and one for the tutor.

Case study 2 – Joanne (a woman wanting to become a registered child-minder and also return to study, and whose children were now teenagers).

★ an appropriate assessment

Joanne came to an adult basic education daytime group. The tutor was able to complete with her an individual profile of her reading tasks and skills (as in 'Make an individual profile', page 36) in a 45-minute chat over coffee.

★ the main problem areas

For reading, these were self-esteem, reading for information, understanding the jargon in the child-care professions, using the library, understanding self-employment material on insurance and tax.

Joanne had earlier in the year started to attend a women's return-to-study course at the local FE college. She had a lively interest in many things and expressed herself well verbally but had no formal qualifications from her schooldays. She found the course very hard going and was not able to keep up with the reading and writing required. She gave up the course, even though it meant forfeiting a large course fee. It appeared that other members of the course were women with A-levels etc, so Joanne felt at a social and academic disadvantage in discussions.

★ where to start

It was agreed to start by looking at texts concerned with child-care (DHSS leaflets, health education leaflets, Toy Library Association magazines, the NNEB certificate syllabus from the FE college etc). These could provide practice in reading skills in general.

★ how to proceed

Joanne had individual help in the ABE group from a volunteer tutor. The tutor would supervise the work programme and provide group activities which Joanne would join in, eg letter-writing, word games, computer reading games.

★ the targets

1 an increase in confidence in reading, writing and maths (long term)
2 completion of the coursework and project for the RSA Certificate of Continuing Education (long term – possibly one or two years)
3 finding information to get started on the project on child-care (short and long term)
4 widening her understanding of words in general, especially to do with child-care (short and long term)

★ timescale

Joanne wanted to register as a child-minder as soon as possible. There was no problem with her application, so she would be registered in a couple of months, but she wanted to be able to interpret 'official' letters and leaflets and forms immediately. The ABE group met for 90 minutes once a week. Joanne wanted to do work at home as well. She aimed to complete the RSA Certificate in one year.

★ who else was involved

After a while, Joanne attended two ABE daytime groups in the week. The two group co-ordinating tutors met and discussed how to share out the work involved for the certificate between the two groups. They agreed to split the work so that group 1 worked on maths and project, and group 2 on reading and writing course work.

★ resources

The ABE groups had a wide variety of books and worksheets available. Child-care material came from DHSS, health education local office, Toy Library Association, health visitor etc. Both groups met in a school setting, one in a classrooom, one in an adult education wing of a school. One group made coffee with a kettle in the corner, the other met in the staff/coffee room half-way through the session.

★ the best way to work

Joanne agreed to fit in with the pattern of work of the ABE groups – individual work and group activities almost equally balanced. She was able to do about half the work on her own, but needed individual help for the other half.

What actually happened

★ start from what the learner can do already

Starting from the forms and leaflets Joanne felt familiar with, the tutor was able to ask her to look for particular words, explain words, summarise parts of the texts, and practise spellings of crucial words. Then they worked on writing an official letter where Joanne knew what she wanted to say (to social services, Inland Revenue etc) and used this as proofreading practice.

★ find, make or adapt teaching material

Apart from ABE published material, there were the leaflets etc. They also used computer reading and spelling games, word games like Scrabble or word dominoes.

★ be prepared to change direction

Half-way through the first year, Joanne's husband was sent by his firm to work abroad for nine months. She accompanied him but was determined to rejoin the groups afterwards. The group tutors were able to provide a limited amount of distance learning material, eg audio tapes, exchange of letters etc.

★ monitor progress regularly

The two groups used different methods of monitoring. One used a checklist of skills which was completed at regular dates. The other asked members to complete at the end of every session the answers to the questions

'What have you done this session? Were there any problems?

How did you tackle them?'

Finding and adapting resources

'Unofficial' resources

Almost anything can be a resource for reading – words are everywhere. Materials should ideally be provided by the learner, and in any case must be relevant to them.

⫟ Activity

Resources

Add about ten extra resources to this list. Bear in the mind the people you work with and choose items that might be relevant to them.

newspapers and magazines

instruction leaflets

signs

telephone message pads

letters, postcards

bills

stock lists

catalogues

invoices

timesheets

expenses claim forms

forms

timetables

directories

computer screens

posters

adverts

exam papers, syllabuses

Our thoughts

The range is endless. It is best developed with the learners.

'Official' resources

At all levels, the best resources are those the learners want to and need to read. The session plans give advice on and show how to use material, published or 'found', to work on all the reading strategies.

For beginning readers

If someone is at the beginning level of reading, most published 'reading skills' books are too full of words. Beware the books that were obviously written for children, as well as what look like easy to use books of spelling 'rules'. They usually take reading away from the context of real life and do not offer the learner the chance to practise the words they want to read.

Using the learner's own writing (or words dictated to you as scribe) to develop reading at this level is particularly valuable. This can just as easily be a set of instructions on setting up some machinery as a personal letter to a sister in Australia.

Many literacy schemes and publishers produce adult reading material at this level — often individuals and groups of adult learners have written their memories down in the form of very short books.

For improving and fairly competent readers

Using the learner's own writing is again very valuable, especially for proofreading, a vital skill in jobs where writing, typing, and word processing are required. But it can also be used to develop the other reading skills.

A greater variety of published material is useful at these levels. But it still needs choosing with care.

At all levels

Computer programs can provide practice in reading in a way that print often cannot easily do. Games and puzzles may relieve the pressure of 'reading practice'.

Some useful guides to what is available include:

Literacy and numeracy materials: a guide, MSC, 1988

Resources, ALBSU, 1987

ALBSU newsletters, quarterly

These all contain information on current materials, books, videos, tapes, software and games, names of publishers and distributors, some reviews and notes on who the material is suitable for. They also give prices and notes on photocopiable material.

A template for individual sessions

In any session, whether five minutes, 30 minutes, one or two hours, it is useful to have a framework for the session — a template.

One suggested template for a one-hour session is:

Tutor

★	PREPARATION	30-45 mins

Learners and tutor together

★	REVIEW 1	5 mins
★	INTRODUCTION	5 mins
★	ACTIVITIES	40 mins (including break)
★	REVIEW 2	5 to 10 mins

Tutor

★	PLAN	15 mins

This is what might go into each slot in the template:

PREPARATION

• consider learners' and tutor's comments on how things went last time

• note the aims and objectives of this session

• collect materials

• make and duplicate a worksheet or handout

• book a room, video, OHP etc in advance

REVIEW 1

• talk about how things went last time

• discuss what went well and why

• agree to work on any problems that came up

INTRODUCTION

• explain what is planned for this session

ACTIVITIES

• do reading, writing, talking, games, puzzles

• vary the pace so that learners succeed in every task

• break in the middle for a breather or coffee

• agree on 'homework' if appropriate

REVIEW 2

• talk about, and ask learners to record, if appropriate, how things went this time

• agree on work for next time

PLAN

• make notes on this session, including learners' and tutor's comments

• briefly plan next session

The 'templates' are suggestions for a way of working. You may have your own methods already working successfully, but if you are fairly new to this kind of teaching it is well worth deciding on a flexible, structured approach of the sort suggested above.

YOUR TEACHING STRATEGY

This section lists a number of things to think about for each of the attitudes readers need, the knowledge they can acquire and the skills they can use. You can help learners to use all the ideas here at any level and in any learning session.

Attitudes

Confidence

The kind of experiences you had while trying the activities earlier in the book will have shown you that a confident reader, however hard the reading task is, has the confidence to

★ read familiar texts

★ try new and complex words

★ make mistakes and learn from them

★ stop when they've had enough.

The tutor can help learners towards confident reading by explaining to them how people learn to read — the knowledge they acquire and the skills they develop — there is no mystery about the process and it should be explained to learners.

Adults also like to be in control of their learning, to set the pace and use the methods that suit them.

The tutor's role is also to give realistic encouragement — the sessions that you will be able to provide may not work miracles. But reading has to be seen in perspective. For some people it is essential all the time, for others it is useful on certain occasions only. It all depends on the individual — some people may be quite happy to live without it. Everyone is entitled to feel happy with the level of reading that suits them.

Purpose

A learner may have a very individual purpose for reading. For instance, someone who breeds tropical fish may be very competent at extracting the information they need from the specialist magazine on guppies, but later in the day be struggling with a note from their supervisor at work.

People's purposes may coincide, especially where they have to work together and read safety instructions or guidelines on working practices.

Readers also need to be aware of the purpose of the person who wrote what they are reading. This may be to impress, persuade, instruct, encourage, prejudice, complain, congratulate, admonish etc. People may find it fairly easy to work out the mood of someone's spoken words but have more difficulty with the written words. Learners and tutors can discuss what lies behind written words at any level.

Everyone has some purpose in reading — the tutor can find the learner's strengths and build on them.

Feeling at ease

'One of the most formidable impediments . . . at all levels of reading, is anxiety.'
(Essays into literacy, Frank Smith, Heinemann Educational Books, 1983)

There are many ways a tutor can help here.

Ideally, you can give the learner time to relax with reading, a low-stress setting, and a wide range of materials and resources or media. In practice you will probably manage only some of these. But there are some things to bear in mind:

★ some people may find reading aloud in front of others stressful or embarrassing, so anxiety gets in the way of memory and skills; anyway, hardly anyone ever needs to do it

★ reading need not always be done sitting upright at a schoolroom type table

★ reading is not just done from books

Here are some things you can do about those:

★ ask learners to read aloud only for specific purposes, eg reading to children, reading out instructions for others, making a speech, announcing some information, asking questions from a quiz or survey

★ read simultaneously with the learner, gradually letting them take over

★ encourage learners to read to themselves and observe or ask whether they have understood

★ if appropriate, rearrange the furniture or find more comfortable chairs and tables

★ encourage learners to read at home when they feel comfortable, eg with music, tv, radio on — reading should not be torture

★ look at a variety of media; print, handwritten pieces, audio and video, games, computer software, photographs, film, tv, diagrams, symbols, maps, maths

★ record some reading the learner wants to do onto tape

★ make up games or use published games; try computer games

★ use the learner's own writing to read, so that they know it is their own and that they are not at the mercy of an unknown writer.

Knowledge

Learners do need some basic theory about reading. Competent readers take many basic principles so much for granted that they are largely unconscious of the fact that, for example, words go left to right on a line and that letters have names and sounds associated with them.

Learners can use this basic theory as they develop their reading skills.

Left to right; top to bottom

For some people this is a problem, maybe because of eyesight or familiarity with another script.

One thing learners may like to do at the very beginning is to run a finger, ruler, piece of paper along under the line they are reading – it helps to concentrate the eye on the line and may help with the flow of reading. Scanning back to the beginning of the next line is often a problem for some people, but having some reference point, like a pencil, can help a great deal.

The tutor can help by encouraging the learner to use the method that suits them best, and help them to discard any feeling of it being silly.

Once learners are happy with the way the text is laid out allow them to develop their own method of keeping their eyes where they want them to be. Learners should also be encouraged to use other clues from the page, so sticking to this system too rigidly is not helpful.

When confident readers read, their eyes move erratically over the words gathering clues to the meaning as quickly as possible. So bear this in mind when you are helping beginning readers follow the general direction of text.

Structure words

The 100 most common words in English is given in Handout 2, 'One hundred key words'. They make up half of all the reading material learners are ever likely to meet. You can try counting these words in any text that is available – try comparing a piece from *The Sun* with a piece from *The Independent* and they will show a surprising amount in common.

These words don't carry meaning themselves; they hold together the words that do give the text its meaning – they have been called 'mortar' or 'link' words for that reason. They are best memorised so that learners can recognise them in a flash.

Similar ones such as 'of', 'for', 'from', and 'if' can be given to learners in different sequences; they will soon get quicker at recognising them quickly. Learners can look for certain ones in a piece of text and underline them. Or initially they can be practised by using flash cards, ie written on cards and held up for a few moments while you say the words. The learner then can be asked to pick out particular words when the cards are turned face up. You can do this with just two cards at first, then any number.

Social words

There are some common ones 'in context' in Handout 3, 'Everyday words'. They are words always seen in context so they usually contain visual clues, other than the actual letters themselves. You can practise these in the same way as the structure words. Learners and tutors can also discuss what clues these signs give them for the meanings of words, and perhaps transfer those to other instances of the same words.

It is encouraging to many beginning readers to realise that they know more of these than they at first think. So they are often good building blocks for the learner's confidence.

Letter names, and the alphabet sequence

Letter names (ay, bee, cee etc) are used most commonly to spell words out; names on the phone etc. But words very rarely sound like the sum of their letter names, eg 'who' 'double you aitch owe'.

Some learners may also be unsure of the sequence of the alphabet. Since many directories and indexes rely on the alphabet, is important to be confident in using it. You can practise this in many ways, for example:

★ use Scrabble letters to arrange in sequence

★ start with an M and ask learners to place letters either side of it

★ open a dictionary at random and ask for the previous and following letters to the one on the page

★ practise the alphabet forwards and backwards so that learners can flick either way through a directory

★ cut up any word and ask the learner to rearrange the letters in alphabetical order.

The shape of letters and words

Beginning writers may be helped to learn how letters are formed. But it is also important in reading to be confident about the difference between capital and lower case letters, between those letters which many people confuse ('b' and 'd', 'n' and 'u'), and between styles of handwriting or print. Many people confuse capitals and lower case letters in their writing, and can usually proofread them as errors if they are helped to look closely.

Words too have their own distinctive shape. If you use the edge of a piece of paper to cover up the bottom half of the words on this line you will probably recognise familiar words by their shape. Words also have an overall shape, which helps people distinguish between eg 'thought' and 'through'. Sometimes learners will be distinguishing between words of different lengths, eg in 'battalion' and 'bit' or between words where only one letter is different, eg in 'bat' and 'bet'.

Learners and tutors can discuss what shapes they see in words that make them distinctive − whatever emerges may help others.

Letter sounds and patterns

Many practice books on spelling group these into 'word families', but practising any reading or spelling out of the context of what the learner wants or needs is unhelpful. Plenty of letter patterns can be found in the learner's own writing or any words anywhere.

Your aim is to help learners understand that one letter can have a variety of different sounds depending on its position in the word or what other letter or letters are next to it. They need to be able to distinguish between different letter combinations. You can look for letter patterns in materials that are relevant to the learner. They can record the words they find in a pocket word book or index card system, maybe in the context of a sentence.

Syllables, parts of words, emphasis

Syllables are like the musical beat of a word. Breaking down unfamiliar words into syllables can help learners to pronounce them. The emphasis point helps here too.

It also helps to break down words according to where they look breakable – that may be something to do with the spelling. Learners, including beginning readers, are often very good at this. For instance:

> 'beginning' breaks visually at 'beg-inn-ing' though aurally it sounds better as 'be-ginn-ing'.

People often find that once they have the first one or two syllables or parts of a word they can predict the rest.

It is also useful to recognise prefixes and suffixes, (eg un-, mis-, re-, dis-, sub-, and -ment, -able, -ing, -er, -ly, -ed etc). This is both for their letter patterns and their meanings which they add to the root words.

One useful exercise is to take all the words from a piece of text with prefixes and suffixes, separate and mix up those parts of the words and the root parts, and ask the learner to put them together again and talk about the possible combinations.

You can also blank out every occurrence of a common syllable in a piece of text and ask the learner to fill them in.

This needs to be handled carefully because as you have seen, successful reading involves a wide range of knowledge and skills. Knowing about syllables and parts of words is only one of the clues readers use; it can easily be overemphasised and the learner can lose confidence.

Grammar

The word frightens many people because it is associated with much specialised jargon. The terms are not necessary because the function of a word in a text is clear. But if learners *want* to learn the grammar that is a good reason for explaining it. These are the terms that could be helpful for those who are interested:

> 'sentence' – knowing where one begins and ends
>
> 'vowels and consonants' – for the way they affect one another in spelling (not necessary for reading)
>
> 'singular and plural' – or 'one and more than one'
>
> 'question', 'command' – that is, the intention of the writer
>
> 'noun, verb, adjective, adverb' – again only for those who want to know about them.

Everyone speaks with a well developed grammar, or structure of the language, of their own. This may vary between groups of people and individuals, but it is never the case that someone's grammar is absolutely wrong. When written down, it may be inappropriate for its audience, but people can learn to adapt their writing to the circumstances. If you are discussing the structure of any piece of writing or text, beware of too much jargon because it gets in the way. Certainly as far as reading is concerned everyone who can talk has enough 'natural' grammar to allow them to predict the correct parts of speech.

Punctuation and layout

Learners need to know about punctuation and layout because they make a difference to meaning, and both certainly make texts easier or harder to read.

Here again, too much jargon is often unhelpful. Full stops, commas, question marks and perhaps colons are the most useful at all levels, especially in proofreading. An understanding of paragraphs is also useful; so are the conventional layouts of a business letter, in-house reports, memos etc.

Punctuation and layout are further clues for learners to recognise; they allow easier access to the meaning.

Use of reading skills

Predicting — getting words, meaning and purpose from the context

It may be tempting for a tutor to insist on everything being read correctly, sometimes from a genuine concern that the learner will be confused if it is not. But, as the main purpose of reading is to get at the meaning, it does not matter if the learner makes a 'mistake' as long as the meaning is not affected. Confident readers make 'mistakes' but don't know unless the sense of the text is lost.

Predicting/guessing what comes next may apply to, words and meaning of words, or whole chunks of text. For instance, you can make a collection of phrases or first sentences of a variety of texts, as suggested in *Extending reading skills* (ALBSU, 1987) and ask the learners to match them up with the type of text, eg guidebook, epitaph, detective story, etc.

The cloze procedure (examples are given in this book) is particularly helpful here for developing the skill of predicting.

Another aspect of this is the skill to predict the argument in a text, the way the writer is thinking. The reader has the advantage if they can keep in step with the writer and not be taken in (unless they want to be, as in for example a 'whodunnit' story).

Reading between the lines

Everything that is written comes from the mind of the writer, and every reader is entitled to use their own judgment on what the writer means, on what is fact and on what is opinion. Beginning readers may need help from a tutor reading something with or for them, but they are no less able to judge what, for example, some advertisers are trying to persuade people to do, than more competent readers are.

There is a wide variety of material that you can use to help learners develop these critical skills – letters, advertisements, publicity material, estate agents' literature, newspaper articles, etc.

Skimming and scanning

Skimming means running your eyes over a whole page or whole text to get the general feel of it. It means reading any titles or subheadings, initial sentences either in paragraphs or sections or chapters, final sentences and perhaps selected bits in between. The idea is to get a general idea of the content but not the detailed meaning. If your learners are involved in any studying skimming is a useful skill to learn.

Scanning means looking for particular facts, words, sentences, headings, paragraphs, sections etc. It means picking them out for their meaning which may be central to the whole text or for information to lead you on to other parts of the book or manual or because that is all you need to know. The skill is in being able to read selectively and not be side-tracked by things that are not important. Again this is a valuable skill for learners who are doing some other form of studying or who need to get at particular bits of information in a job but don't need to read everything.

Using a dictionary and reference material

Tutors cannot take it for granted that people are happy using a dictionary. Many learners know that if you cannot spell a word, you don't know where to look for it in the dictionary. So it is something to bear in mind at all levels, and a skill to encourage at all levels while learners are becoming more confident with letter patterns for instance.

Some learners use a dictionary like a thesaurus – they look up a word they do know how to spell, eg 'house' when they want to find 'accommodation', hope that 'accommodation' is given next to 'house', and then look up the exact meaning of the one they wanted in the first place. They could be encouraged to actually use an alphabetical thesaurus.

It is useful to have a variety of dictionaries for learners to look at and choose the one they feel most at ease with. They vary so much in print style, layout and information, that the choice in the shops is bewildering. It is worth discussing the reasons for choosing a particular one.

Practising alphabetical order (as above) is a vital skill for dictionaries and reference books of all kinds.

Learners can sort out groups of words or names, from one or two to a long list, according to the initial, then subsequent letters. It is usually best if these are taken from their own writing or own needs.

Reference material is not all in books. People can learn how to gain access to filing systems, computer indexes, microfiches, and find information on audio and video cassettes. All involve a lot of reading, and may be used at all levels.

Proofreading

Proofreading *is* a skill of reading but one that is associated with writing, either the learner's or someone else's. It involves very detailed reading, and requires the reader to know more about *writing* than reading as it is the writing that is being checked.

Learners need mostly to proofread their own work, rather than other people's. So using their own writing will be more helpful than producing examples from a completely different source. But it may be illuminating to show learners examples of writing that has come from other parts of the company or college that has not been proofread and to discuss why it matters.

Ask for help if they want it

Learners will often need to ask for help, but asking is a skill. Asking the wrong person, asking the wrong question or asking in the wrong way can cause embarrassment and loss of confidence. And if the learner is in control of their learning, they will need to be the ones who decide when to ask for help, however frustrating that may be for you.

You are able to support and encourage learners in this area. They will be in other situations where they will need help with their reading; asking for any sort of help is difficult, especially in new jobs or other new situations, so questions relating to reading are likely to be very hard. You can give them a safe environment where they can discuss how they feel about asking for help and practise ways of doing it.

Choose what they want to read

Unless learners express no preference they should be encouraged to select their own reading material. Selecting and rejecting are skills and important ones if they are not going to feel discouraged by choosing material that is at the wrong level or does not provide the information they want.

Looking at a few pages and counting the number of words that are too difficult will give an idea of level. As a guide five difficult words are about the maximum a reader can cope with, even with help. Reading a few bits to see if it makes sense is a good idea too.

Checking that the information is the most up to date available may be important, as well as skimming (reading headings, introductory sentences etc) to see if the content is right.

Having confidence to select and reject without feeling hurried is another skill that can be practised during reading sessions.

As with other aspects of reading the learner needs to be in control and this includes deciding what is appropriate to read. There will be occasions when choice is less possible – with safety instructions, operating instructions, other course material or things needed for work. But learners are most likely to want to read the items they need for work.

The session plans give suggestions for discussing the issues here at all levels. If you ensure that you are encouraging confidence, purpose and a feeling of ease, then you are likely to find that the rest is relatively easy.

SESSION PLANS

This section includes suggested session plans:

★ two for beginning readers

★ two for improving readers

★ two for fairly competent readers

★ two group sessions for mixed groups

★ one group session for fairly competent and competent readers.

The words 'beginning', 'improving', 'fairly competent' and 'competent' here mean roughly:

'beginning' – from someone who can read nothing, to someone who can read basic signs (TOILET etc), their own and family names, familiar shops and tv programmes, and perhaps know the alphabet

'improving' – someone who can read road and public signs and some simple instructions, food tins, newspaper headlines, bills and some leaflets

'fairly competent' – someone who can read most official forms but may have difficulty with the meaning, read newspaper articles, have some knowledge of punctuation and layout, can recognise many wrong spellings and can use a dictionary or directory

'competent' – someone who can read forms or reports for information, recognise wrong spellings and use dictionaries, use manuals and reference books, read novels and lengthy newspaper articles, but needs help in speeding up with all those.

The people you know will not fall easily into one of those groups – people and reading are just not like that. The 'levels' are very general guidelines.

Each session follows the suggested 'template' of

> PREPARATION
>
> REVIEW 1
>
> INTRODUCTION
>
> ACTIVITIES
>
> REVIEW 2
>
> PLAN

This may or may not suit you as a framework. It is just a suggestion. Above all, be prepared to change direction when you are following the learner's lead. If someone comes to a session wanting to go through a leaflet on the right to buy their own council house, then that is what they need to read. You may have agreed together last time to work on scanning, and you may have prepared work at great length — but that can always be used another time. Besides, the work on scanning is probably waiting for you in the right to buy leaflet.

SESSION 1 — beginning reader

PREPARATION — tutor

Review   how things went last time

Aims   to increase learners' confidence with reading safety signs at work

Objectives   at the end of the session, the learner should be able to read some relevant health and safety signs

Materials   pens, paper, learner's pocket word book, safety at work leaflets (including signs) relevant to learner's job, signs on cards/photographs also relevant to learner's job

photocopy of signs — Handout 1, 'Safety signs', might be appropriate

worksheet — sign words with gaps to fill

homework — wordsearch with safety words in it

Arrangements   make sure a room and coffee is available.

REVIEW 1 — learner and tutor

Discuss   homework, if appropriate what went well last time; any problems from last time; when to work on those problems

INTRODUCTION

Explain   you will be working on safety signs the learner needs to read at work

ACTIVITIES

Discuss   which ones learner knows already and which are difficult

Find out   how the learner has learnt to read some signs already

Agree	to build on those and tackle, say, three new words in the session
Do it	1 Look at signs. Read with the learner and ask them to guess meaning from the context eg FIRE EXIT – MUST BE KEPT ..... SWITCH OFF ...... HIGHLY ....
	2 Write word on three strips of card in large letters.
	3 Discuss the letter patterns in the word and where else the words are found.
	4 Look at the shape of the word – discuss distinctive features eg in INFLAMMABLE the two MMs could look like flames in a fire.
	5 Ask learner to write the word and say it, then write it in own word book (ie using alphabetical index).
	6 Talk about signs and symbols – visual clues eg shape or colour of sign (circle, triangle, red, yellow etc)
	7 Talk about the meaning of words if that is appropriate, eg 'prohibition', 'mandatory' which may not be clear to the learner.
Break	at some point, for a chat, coffee etc
Do more	8 eg wordsearch using safety sign words.

REVIEW 2

Discuss how things went and what to do next time, eg looking for those words in the safety leaflet and reading some of the leaflet instructions, eg on fire drill.

PLAN – tutor

Make notes on what happened, whether aims and objectives fulfilled, on pacing, and brief plan for next time, eg making sure there is a copy of the safety leaflet, making a 'pairs' game with the safety words in pairs (one in lower case letters, one in capitals).

SESSION 2 – beginning reader

PREPARATION – tutor

Review	how things went last time
Aims	to use the learner's own writing to read

Objectives	at the end of this session the learner should be able to read some of own writing, feel confident about it and have a few new words in own pocket workbook
Materials	pens, pencils, paper, scissors, pocket word book
Arrangements	room and coffee

REVIEW 1 – learner and tutor

Discuss	homework, if appropriate what went well last time; any problems from last time; when to work on those problems

INTRODUCTION

Explain	you will be asking the learner to talk about something eg their work and writing down for them what they want to say. Explain this is because this will help with reading words they need and also because you are interested.

ACTIVITIES

Discuss	something of interest to the learner
Write	some of what the learner said – let them decide what you write
Agree	you will look at this and use it for reading practice
Do it	1 Read it out to the learner then along with them if reading aloud is appropriate. 2 Write it out again, identically, and cut up and mix up the sentences. Ask the learner to match them with the original. 3 Ask the learner to look for particular words, particular letters, parts of words, letter patterns etc. 4 Ask the learner to put the words they want into their word book, ie using alphabetical index
Break	for a chat, coffee 5 Use the passage or some of it for writing practice – read through again, together, then dictate it to the learner to write, pacing it appropriately 6 Homework: write two of the longer words on a piece of paper and ask the learner to find words within those words, using letters that are in sequence

and next to each other. For example 'mark' is all right from 'supermarket', but 'make' isn't.

REVIEW 2

Discuss how things went and what to do next time, eg doing more writing or reading a note about work from a supervisor.

PLAN — tutor

Make notes on what happened, whether aims and objectives fulfilled, and brief plan for next time, eg getting an example of a supervisor's note from work.

SESSION 3 — improving reader

PREPARATION — tutor

Review	how things went last time
Aims	to help learner with structure words
Objectives	at the end of the session the learner should know more structure words
Materials	highlighter pen, paper and card, pen, learner's pocket word book, brochure/adverts for something brought by learner (eg car, motorbike, shoes, anything) Handout 2, 'One hundred key words' and Handout 3, 'Everyday words'
Arrangements	room, coffee etc

REVIEW 1 — learner and tutor

Discuss	how things went last time
	what went well last time
	when to work on any problems

INTRODUCTION

Explain	you will be looking for the key words in pieces of print to do with their interest and brought by them; you will also be practising 'scanning' for the 'structure' words

ACTIVITIES

Read   1 the text, with the learner and ask them to read it or part of it, to themselves

Discuss   2 any part which you or the learner do not understand

3 the one hundred key words — explain they make up half the words in any piece of writing anyone will have to read; start with the first 12, then the next 20 to establish how many the learner is happy with

Look for 4 the first one, two or three, or the first 12, according to how confident the learner is in the material they have brought; ask learner to highlight words every time they occur; discuss how many there are

5 continue with an appropriate number of key words, depending on how many the learner is happy with — it may be just one, it could be the lot if you have worked on this before

6 Give out copies of handout 2, 'One hundred key words' — they may like to put ones they are not sure of into their pocket word book or card index

Practise 7 any two or three key words the learner is not sure of — write them on cards, ask the learner to say which one says eg 'the', which one 'was' , which one 'said'

8 turn the cards face down, ask the learner to turn them up one by one and say the word

talk about how the learner is recognising these — helping them to decide what works best for them

Break   for a chat, coffee, etc

Do more   9 use handout 3, 'Everyday words' for reading practice.

REVIEW

Discuss how things went and what to do next time, eg looking for structure words in another text, going over this work again, or look for different structure words in the same text.

PLAN

Make notes on what happened. Make a brief plan for next time, including what materials may be needed.

SESSION 4 – improving reader

PREPARATION – tutor

Review   how things went last time

Aims   to increase the learner's reading fluency by using
              simultaneous reading and tape recording

Objectives at the end of the session, the learner should be able
              to read ahead, miss out words and come back to
              them, predict meaning from the context

Materials   tape recorder and blank cassette, pen, pencil, thick
              felt tip pen, highlighter pen, paper, card, learner's
              pocket word book, text the learner wants to read

Arrangements suitable socket for tape recorder, comfortable place
               to sit while recording, coffee etc.

REVIEW 1 – learner and tutor

Discuss   what went well last time

              any problems

              when to work on those problems

INTRODUCTION

Explain   you will be looking at the item the learner has
              provided and will be helping the learner to read
              through without stopping; you will be reading the
              information on to tape so that the learner can use it
              at home – the learner does not need to record their
              own voice unless they want to

ACTIVITIES

Discuss   1 what the learner already knows about the subject
              of the item they have brought in, why they chose that
              piece and how they want to use it in the future

              2 write down some of the clue words to look for

Read   3 through with or for the learner slowly; ask the
              learner to highlight the clue words they do recognise

Discuss	4 what makes it easy or hard to read; make a list, eg
	print size
	meaning of words
	layout
	explain any of the meanings the learner is not sure of
Find	5 some words the learner did not know and write them on cards to work on later
Record	6 the whole text, slowly but naturally, with the learner following the text (using an aid if appropriate)
	7 ask learner to write the words they want to remember in their pocket word book
Break	for chat, coffee etc
Read	8 through again, but stop at words you know the learner knows so that they can fill them in
	9 through again but stop at random so that the learner can predict what comes next — but only if you are sure they have a clear idea in mind of the overall flow of the text
	10 try it again if it worked, stopping at different places
Homework	11 ask the learner to listen to your recording at home and follow the text at the same time, read along with it and if possible record it themselves

Other suggestions:

★ use some written cloze exercises

★ ask questions on the text for the learner to write or record answers to

★ ask the learner to explain (writing or recording or saying) in their own words what is in the text.

REVIEW 2

Discuss how things went and how you both felt about recording your own voices — both tutor and learner may feel awkward so you can share the discomfort.

Agree what to do next time, eg looking at the difficult words and finding other strategies to tackle (sounding out letters, breaking up into parts, looking for letter patterns etc), looking at other instructions the learner needs or wants to do, or more of the same. Agree on what materials might be needed.

PLAN — tutor

Make notes on what happened, and plan briefly for next time.

Some suggestions: make a simplified version of the text if that is needed, use the learner's own recording or writing to work on, make a 'pairs' game with any specialised words on cards (see 'Games and puzzles' in Section 4, 'Bits and pieces').

SESSION 5 — fairly competent reader

PREPARATION — tutor

Review	how things went last time
Aims	to help the learner become confident in using dictionaries and directories
Objectives	at the end of the session the learner should be more confident with alphabetical order, be familiar with other aspects of using a dictionary and be able to find their way round some directories
Materials	pens, pencils, paper, card, learner's pocket word book, choice of dictionaries, thesaurus, any directories chosen by the learner, Handout 4, 'Dictionaries and directories'
Arrangements	room and coffee, availability of library or access to reference books in office etc.

REVIEW 1 — learner and tutor

Discuss	what went well last time; any problems; when and how to work on those problems

INTRODUCTION

Explain	you will be looking at how to use dictionaries and directories, at what's involved, and then working out the learner's own reminder sheet

ACTIVITIES

Discuss
1 which dictionary or thesaurus the learner finds easiest to use and why, eg clear and contrasting print, different colours, with or without phonetic spellings, with or without illustrations, pocket sized, etc

2 what you need to know to be able to use a dictionary, eg alphabet, letter sounds, letter patterns, root words, etc

Practise
3 knowledge of the alphabet – eg which letter is at the beginning, the end, which ones are roughly in the middle, which one comes just before T, how does it go forwards, how backwards? etc; ask the learner to open the dictionary at any page and say which letter comes before and after etc

Talk about
4 words the learner wants to look up – how can they do this?

Do it
5 find those words, look at the spelling and meaning, discuss any oddities

Break
chat, coffee, flick through other dictionaries

Extend
6 explain you use the same skills with directories, catalogues etc – make a list of those the learner wants to use

7 discuss any different skills they demand, eg indexes (by subject or alphabetical, trade and domestic, where placed in the book, use of numbers); why they are used, advantages and disadvantages

Practise
8 those aspects the learner finds difficult.

REVIEW 2

Look at handout 4, 'Dictionaries and directories' and help learners fill it in if they want. Discuss how things went and what to do next time, eg using a dictionary or thesaurus to edit the learner's writing, or where to find technical or specialist dictionaries, or how to use the library effectively etc

PLAN – tutor

Make notes on what happened this time and what the learner would like to do next time. Check on materials.

SESSION 6 — fairly competent reader

PREPARATION — tutor

Review	how things went last time
Aims	to help the learner develop the skill of proofreading their own writing
Objectives	at the end of this session the learner should be more able to use proofreading and editing skills
Materials	pens, pencils, paper or typewriter and white-out fluid, or word processor, learner's pocket word book, dictionary
Arrangements	room, coffee, typewriter, word processor etc.

REVIEW 1 — learner and tutor

Discuss	what went well last time; any problems; when and how to work on those problems;

INTRODUCTION

Explain	you are asking the learner to do some writing that they want to do, eg an application letter, and then work on that to practise the skills of proofreading etc.

ACTIVITIES

Write	1 ask the learner to write, type or key a first draft of anything
Discuss	2 how to skim for wrong spellings and do look them up in a dictionary, or use a spelling checker on the word processor
	3 what is missing (addresses, date, any words etc)
	4 when and where capital letters are appropriate
	5 use of appropriate language
	6 ways of making it easy to read — layout, paragraphs, punctuation etc
Break	chat, coffee etc
Discuss	7 does it say what the learner wants it to say?; is there anything else to change, add, take out?; what

effect does the learner want to have on the reader?

Write   8   write, type or key a final copy.

REVIEW 2

Work out together the points the learner wants to remember about checking their own writing. Personal notes to themselves are better than general guidelines. Write/type/print these.

Agree on what to work on next time. It may be just the same or something completely different − follow the learner's lead.

PLAN − tutor

Note how things went this time. Briefly plan for next time.

SESSION 7 − mixed group

PREPARATION − tutor

Review
How did things go last time? Is there a particular learner who would like more work on last session's theme? Did one learner help another in a particular way and can they work together again?

Aims
to use a newspaper article on a local issue to stimulate discussion, expression of ideas, and a source for the study of reading skills at a variety of levels

Objectives
at the end of the session, learners should know how to use a newspaper article to practise reading skills that they want; also have produced their own writing/tape/ notes/cartoon etc for others in the group to read

Materials
copies of the same newspaper, photocopies of the story, the same story in different papers, pens, pencils, paper, card, scissors, glue, dictionaries, tape recorder and blank cassette; some materials could be prepared by the tutor beforehand, eg photocopy of article with words blanked out for prediction exercise, photocopy for looking for key words, suggestions on dictionary use, questions on the text, suggestions for writing on the issues, long words from the article to find 'words within words', activity on where to find out more information about a particular issue, the origin of some names in the text, a search for prefixes and suffixes, ie any kind of activity that suits the people in the group

| *Arrangements* | use of photocopier, tables to cut and stick on, socket for tape recorder, chairs for everyone, coffee etc. |

REVIEW 1 — learners and tutor

| *Discuss* | what went well last time; any problems; when and how to work on the problems |

INTRODUCTION

| *Explain* | you are using the newspaper article for discussion and reading practice, and only those who want to can volunteer to read out loud |
| | note that some beginning readers may be very confident to try reading out in the group, and some very competent readers may be extremely shy about doing so — the tutor needs to pace this activity in a sensitive way so that no one feels they are being offended/bored/patronised/asked to do the impossible/made to look foolish |

ACTIVITIES

Break	at some point for a chat, coffee etc
Discuss	1 ask someone or several people to read out some of the article, making sure everyone has the time to follow it through
	2 ensure that everyone has the chance, if they want to, to express their opinions on the article
Suggest	3 ways of using this article as reading practice (see suggestions for tutor-prepared materials above); learners may like to work in pairs or a small group, with or without the tutor, or individually. Some suggestions are:
	individual (beginning reader):
	cut out the headlines or other words and mix and match parts of words or letters
	individual or pair (beginning readers):
	choose some structure words from the article and make up a wordsearch
	individual (improving reader):
	listen to a tape recording of the article made by the

tutor or another learner with questions and gaps
for answers built in

pairs (improving to fairly competent readers):

work on the same cloze exercise and then compare
and discuss answers with the other pair

pairs (fairly to competent readers):

read the article together and make up a dialogue
between reporter and interviewee which might have
led to the article — tape record or write this

pairs or small groups (competent readers):

read two or more accounts of the same story in
different newspapers if they are available — ask
them to write or talk about differences in the
writers' intentions, use of language, layout etc

*NB the above are suggestions for learners working
on their own, with the guidance of one group tutor.
If the members of a group are used to working with
others, you could ask people in one session to make
up worksheets or handouts for other people at
different levels.*

*Note also that beginning readers are just as able as
competent readers to talk about differences between
two or more presentations of an issue. They just need
much more help with the actual reading, so you need
to give them the time and the individual support to
help them towards that.*

Share 4 if appropriate, between pairs or small groups the
activities worked out by others, eg listen to the tape
made by some learners, photocopy the wordsearch
etc.

REVIEW 2

Discuss how things went this time and what to do next, eg with
some learners following up some research at the library into the
issues discussed, some writing their own opinions etc.

PLAN — tutor

Make notes on what happened, who worked well together, any
problems that emerged for anyone. Arrange to photocopy or type
people's work if they want it, etc. Make brief plan for next time.

SESSION 8 — mixed group

PREPARATION — tutor

Review how things went last time

Aims to make effective use of a computer in a mixed group setting for reading practice

Objectives at the end of the session or series of sessions, learners should be confident in using cloze or word game type programs to improve their reading

Materials computer(s), reading program(s), eg those in 'Some resources and sources of help' near the end of this book, pens, pencils, paper, dictionaries, learners' pocket word books, learners' own writing, group tutor or specialist tutor who is familiar with programs

Arrangements computers available, tables for writing, spare disks for learners' writing or input, room, coffee etc.

REVIEW 1 — learners and tutor

Discuss how things went last time — any individual problems or requests and agree when and how to work on those

INTRODUCTION

Explain learners will be working individually, or in twos or threes, to use computer programs on reading; anyone can use a computer but no one will be forced to; say that some reading programs are a good back-up to pen and paper work and can be fun

Discuss any worries people have about using computers, and any benefits some people may have found

ACTIVITIES

Ensure 1 people are familiar with loading programs and using the keyboard — ensure everyone has the support they need, perhaps from a confident member of the group

Set up 2 some cloze type programs, eg *Wordskill* (large letters on screen), *Cloze, Developing tray, Wordplay, Copywrite,* etc; most of these programs allow the user to enter their own text; their own writing at any level, and then make a cloze type exercise out of it

Ensure	3 there is enough time for learners to put in their own text if they are not fast typists — they may need to help each other
Encourage	4 learners to discuss what is happening on the screen — working with someone else can be a great mutual help
	5 people to write down words they would like to check, to use a dictionary or thesaurus etc
Ensure	7 you save learners' work on disk
Break	at some time
Finish	8 with a larger group activity, eg *Muddles* or *Wordsquare* ...
	with *Muddles* or a similar program, the whole group can discuss word order, shapes of words, the logic of an argument, or put in their own sequence of sentences for others to work on, eg jokes or riddles ... with *Wordsquare* learners can compile very simple to very complex wordsearches for others to work on — this may back up other work done in the group on a particular topic.

REVIEW 2

Discuss how things went and what to do next, eg learners may want to use computer programs to practise spelling or number work. Some may want to tackle computer manuals or write some simple instructions for using the programs they found most useful.

PLAN — tutor

Note what happened and briefly plan for next time. Note who worked well together and how the whole group interacted.

SESSION 9 — group of competent readers

PREPARATION — tutor

Review	how things went last time
Aims	to help learners develop their skills in a job or course where a lot of reading is required
Objectives	at the end of the session(s) learners should be able to use and explain some of the skills of skimming and scanning and speed-reading, and to know what

works best for them

Materials	pens, pencils, paper, dictionaries, thesaurus, reference books, library catalogue, examples of reports from learners' jobs, examples of course material
Handout	draw up a summary of what to look for in a report
Arrangements	room, coffee, check if any reports or material are confidential.

REVIEW 1 – learners and tutor

Discuss	what went well last time; any problems; and when and how to work on them

INTRODUCTION

Explain	you will be looking at the material the learners are currently having to read and that the group will be discussing and sharing ideas for more effective reading

ACTIVITIES

Discuss	1 the example you have chosen, either with the whole group or in pairs or small groups

2 share thoughts on:

★ difficulties

★ effect of the report or handbook etc

★ how people have tackled them

★ purpose of the writer

★ how group would improve the examples

Practise 3 strategies that may have emerged, eg:

★ deciding how thoroughly the example needs reading

★ taking in a page at a glance

★ highlighting crucial words

★ marking the margins

* ★ translating the jargon/cliches

* ★ looking for 'Conclusions' or 'Recommendations' before the rest of the report/book

* ★ using the index

* ★ using page headings

4 try those out with familiar material, then unfamiliar; discuss the difference

Break   for a chat, coffee etc

Discuss   5 how to apply those strategies to other reading tasks, eg using the library, reference books, using filing systems

Follow-up   6 by session(s) on report writing when learners know what they find helpful in a report or course material.

REVIEW 2

Talk about how things went this time and what to do next, eg report-writing, using a microfiche or computer indexing system etc.

PLAN – tutor

Make notes on what happened, who worked well together and what to do next. Follow the learners' lead.

4 BITS AND PIECES

CHECKING READING LEVELS

Part of effective teaching is making sure materials are matched to learners' needs.

There are checks that can be applied to texts to find out how easy or difficult they are to read. They are known as 'readability formulas'. You may find it useful to apply one of these formulas to material you want to use with your learners. This section looks at the issues:

★ how readability formulas work

★ what their limitations are

★ where you can find out more.

How they work

They involve counting certain language features such as

★ length of sentences

★ length of words

★ number of common words.

Then calculations are carried out to find out the reading 'level' of the text.

Limitations

Some things are not easy to measure, but they should be taken into account. For example, a text on the geology of the Lake District could score as 'difficult' if one of these formulas were applied. But if the learner was already familiar with some of the geological terms and geographical features it might be easier for *that* learner.

Other features that need to be considered are:

★ what the reader already knows about the subject

★ the content and ideas

★ how it is planned and laid out

★ the grammar and style

★ the words used — whether specialist, abstract, unusual etc.

Readability formulas should never be used on their own. All these other factors should be considered. It is also a good idea to try out the text or parts of it on your learners to find out how they respond.

Find out more

A very useful summary is *Topic sheet 4: readability and readability formulas,* which is available from the Forms Information Centre, Department of Typography and Graphic Communication, University of Reading.

EXAMINATIONS

Reading is the primary skill for any exam or test learners may be taking as part of a course. But there are some 'communications' or 'English' type exams and certificates that you may like to consider for particular learners.

Why use an exam?

For some people exams are not an appropriate aim or goal. Increasing confidence with reading will be all they need to improve their competence and skill. Other learners may like the challenge of an exam because

★ they need it as an entry qualification to a job or course

★ a suitable exam may not have been available to them when they were at school

★ they have failed it once and want to pass for their own satisfaction

★ it will give them confidence to go on to a higher level exam or course

★ it will make them feel better about themselves.

Entering for exams

Examination boards have their own regulations for exams. You need to check

★ if your centre is registered with the board

★ (or) how to register

★ (or) where your nearest centre is

★ what the fees are

★ if there are special rules for disabled candidates

★ dates of examinations

★ dates for registration of candidates

★ the type of exam (multiple-choice, oral, project or combination).

Everything needs to be checked well in advance.

Which exams are available?

These are brief details of some frequently used exams or certificates that you may find helpful. You could also check with your education authority to see if there are any local certificates suitable for recent school leavers.

Associated Examining Board, Stag Hill House, Guildford, Surrey GU2 5XJ, tel (0483) 506506

★ Basic tests in English

Aim: intended to ensure employers recruit a workforce with at least a basic level of skills and knowledge in 12 areas of competence, of which English is one; not a course, and not designed specifically for people with basic reading levels, though often used as a warm-up to GCSE

Skills tested: reading, writing, comprehension

Type of exam: two parts: the first is listening comprehension and then dictation; the second is reading comprehension, eg notice, timetable, placing items in alphabetical order, form-filling, letter-writing

Vocational relevance: intended to prepare students for the world of work

City and Guilds of London Institute (CGLI), 56 Britannia Street, London WC1X 9RG, tel (01) 278 2468

★ Communication Skills (361)

Aim: to develop skills for studying, working, preparing for work, and coping with everyday life

Skills tested: reading, listening, writing, speaking

Type of exam: three levels for each of the above skills levels; course work assessed; students receive a record of achievements on their certificate

Vocational relevance: no special vocational relevance

Department of Employment (jobcentres)

From September 1988 Employment Training replaces all other government sponsored courses.

In Employment Training there is a diagnostic period during which reading, writing and number skills are assessed by training agents.

Contact your local jobcentre for all enquiries.

English Speaking Board (International) Ltd, 32 Norwood Avenue, Southport, Merseyside PR9 7EG, tel (0704) 231366

ESB focuses on the spoken word − oral skills − to give learners of all abilities practice in, and assessment of, their oral skills.

Relevance to reading: practice of oral skills complements reading − communicating printed words forms part of the some of the syllabuses

Vocational relevance: wide range of situations where oral skills are required, including fashion, social care, leisure, TC courses, office skills, police studies, telecommunications, travel and tourism, and many others

Pitmans Examination Institute, Catteshall Manor, Godalming, Surrey GU7 1UU, tel (04868) 25321

★ English Elementary

Aim: to enable students to write and read contemporary English

Skills tested: reading and writing

Type of exam: two hours in four parts: listening comprehension, personal writing, reading comprehension, and grammar

Vocational relevance: part of English and Business Communications syllabus; for people working in or wanting to work in office administration

Royal Society of Arts Examination Board (RSA), John Adam Street, London WC2N 6EZ, tel (01) 930 5115

★ Certificate of Continuing Education

Aim: to provide communication, numeracy and study skills, to increase students' self-confidence and independence and to prepare students for further education or training and employment; the syllabus is followed by many ABE groups

Skills tested: talking with confidence and listening, and reading and study skills, plus number and writing

Type of exam: no formal exams; self-assessment by discussion and agreement with tutors; a profile listing students' competences is given on the certificate

Vocational relevance: no particular vocational relevance

★ Practical Skills Profile Scheme

Aim: *not* a course; acts as a framework to complement existing courses; offers a method of assessment which can be applied in a variety of learning places to record learners' positive achievements

Skills tested: individual schemes cover communication, numeracy and process skills

Type of exam: none; skills competences are listed on the certificate with relevant 'sentences', including many related to reading

Vocational relevance: no particular vocational relevance

Scottish Vocational Education Council (SCOTVEC)

★ National Certificate

Aim: to provide modular, vocationally related training for 16 to 18-year-olds.

Skills tested: wide range of modules described in the *Catalogue of module descriptors* published by SCOTVEC — each module assumes 40 hours learning time.

Type of exam: internal assessments, tests and assignments.

Vocational relevance: according to module(s) selected.

GAMES AND PUZZLES

Games are a valuable way of learning; they can take the pressure off learners by practising reading skills away from the work context. You can play games competitively, or cooperatively in a group or in pairs. Games which involve a degree of chance give all players, tutors and learners, the opportunity to win.

Here are some suggested games and puzzles which include practice in a range of reading skills:

Word games

Scrabble, Lexicon, Boggle, Kan-U-Go, etc.

Domino games

some from educational publishers, but best made up yourself to suit individuals in the group, eg opposites, synonyms, singular/plural, homophones etc.

Board games

any popular game that includes 'chance' cards or similar reading cards; if players are familiar with the game, they will read more than they think they can.

Quiz games

can be played cooperatively, with more competent readers helping others, or playing in teams; eg Trivial Pursuit, Scruples, Quiz Box, Give Us A Clue, or quizzes made up by learners and tutors themselves.

Treasure trails

clues to points in a trail, particularly using local knowledge to find the answers (eg looking at shop, street and house names, reading timetables, maps, getting information from the local library etc); popular if learners compile it themselves.

Crosswords

from newspapers, magazines, books, or home-made by learners or tutors for others; the range is wide and can include any skill or words you choose.

Wordsearches

these are very popular; from newspapers, magazines, etc; from newsagents or home-made as above.

Computer games

both educational and commercial; can be played individually or in small groups; 'logic' or 'mystery' games and 'cloze' type activities may be more fun than 'spelling' type programs.

SOME RESOURCES AND SOURCES OF HELP

Resources for learners

Print

A good life
Alan Gatehouse Project, 1977

Alphabetical order
Printing and Publishing Unit for
Continuing Education (PRU)

An interview
A new man
Dinnerbreak
Ann Chappel, Les Clarke and
Linda Storey
Printing and Publishing Unit for
Continuing Education (PRU)

Asian women speak out: a reader
Amrit Wilson and Julia Naish
National Extension College, 1980

*Assignments 16-19: resources for
language communication*
Barbara Bleiman
Longman, 1986

*Assignments for communication
skills*
Hobsons Publishing, 1987

Atgofion
an adult basic education learner
for Welsh speakers
ALBSU, 1986

At the end of a barge-pole
Keep fit
Kenny Dakin
Beauchamp Lodge

Baselines
(includes software for IBM
compatibles and BBC)
Cambridge Training and
Development Ltd
ALBSU, 1987

Basic dressmaking
Printing and Publishing Unit for
Continuing Education (PRU), 1979

Basic retail assignments
Janet Burley, Cherril Pope and
Grace Wilson
Edward Arnold, 1983

Blacks writing dictionary
T J Hulme, T F Carmody,
J A Hulme
A and C Black, 1972

Cloze books 1 and 2
Printing and Publishing Unit for
Continuing Education (PRU)

Communication themes and skills
Basic Skills Unit Ltd with Martin
Berry
COIC, 1985

Community business pack
Scottish Community Education
Council

*Computer literacy themes and
skills*
Basic Skills Unit Ltd with Stuart
Sillars
COIC, 1985

*Computers in language and
literacy work*
Janet Leonard
ALBSU, 1985

Cuttings collection
various authors
Handprint, 1980 onwards

Dictionary skills
Printing and Publishing Unit for
Continuing Education (PRU)

DIY, Cookery, Budgeting, Driving
(and eight other titles)
Printing and Publishing Unit for
Continuing Education (PRU), 1986

English at work
D O'Sullivan and A Abbott
Collins Educational, 1986

Finding out
Basic Skills Unit Ltd
COIC, 1985

From wages to Windscale
working group of eleven
ALBSU, 1980

From where I stand
Isaac Gordon
Centerprise, 1986

Going where the work is
Isaac Gordon Centerprise, 1979

Health — a basic education pack
three ABE tutors
ALBSU, 1987

How to use a telephone
Printing and Publishing Unit for
Continuing Education (PRU)

How to use your dictionary
Roger Lewis and Martin Pugmire
National Extension College, 1980

*Improve your English through
television*
ALBSU, 1986

Improve your learning
Basic Skills Unit Ltd
Longman, 1984

Improve your reading
Basic Skills Unit Ltd
Longman, 1984

In the pattern
ILEA, 1979

Is it a fair deal?
Jan Marsh
Hobsons Publishing, 1986

Jobs: how to find them
Printing and Publishing Unit for
Continuing Education (PRU)

Looking for work
Janet Swinney
National Extension College, 1985

My job application book
Alan Jamieson
Hobsons Publishing, 1985

Parents and children
five ABE organisers
ALBSU, 1987

Phoning
Andrew Pates and Eileen Mathie
COIC, 1984

Quiz book
Ffion Mercer
Winslow Press, 1983

Reading your Evening Post
Printing and Publishing Unit for
Continuing Education (PRU)

Rocky the woodcarver
(and five other titles)
Merisse Crooks Handprint, 1984-87

*Skills for School Leavers
with learning difficulties*
COIC 1986

Survival pack
Merisse Crooks (ed.)
Handprint, 1986

The ACE spelling dictionary
David Moseley and Catherine Nicol
Learning Development Aids, 1986

Too late
Frances Holden
Gatehouse Project, 1982

Understanding instructions
Val Milburn
Printing and Publishing Unit for Continuing Education (PRU)

Using mail order catalogues
Linda Storey and Bridget Coates
Printing and Publishing Unit for Continuing Education (PRU), 1986

Using newspapers
Printing and Publishing Unit for Continuing Education (PRU)

Using the benefit system
four ABE tutors/organisers
ALBSU, 1984

Using timetables
Printing and Publishing Unit for Continuing Education (PRU)

Using your reference skills
Printing and Publishing Unit for Continuing Education (PRU)

Words about town
Bill Ridgeway
Edward Arnold, 1978

Workfacts
Cambridge Training and Development Ltd COIC, 1987

Working lives (two volumes)
various authors
Centerprise, 1977

Work in progress
Janet Swinney
National Extension College, 1985

Your own car
Basic Skills Unit Ltd with Lesley Crichton
COIC, 1986

Your own motorcycle
Basic Skills Unit Ltd with Phil Garratt and Clive Jones
COIC, 1985

Your own place
Cambridge Training and Development Ltd
COIC, 1986

Games

Biz game
Basic Skills Unit Ltd
COIC

Quiz box
Ffion Mercer
Winslow Press, 1985

Software

Cloze
Michael Trott and Jorg Munschner
Learning and Training Systems Ltd, 1984

Copywrite
Graham Davies and John Higgins
ESM, 1984

Developing tray
ILEA

Fishing game
Cambridge Micro Software
Cambridge University Press, 1986

Fun phonics
Kath Shelton
PAVIC Publications, 1987

Going Solo – Budgeting
COIC

GRASS
Nick Osborne and Phil Turner
Newman College

Matchmaker
C Jones
Wida Software, 1986

Microspecial
Scottish Microelectronics
Development Program
Collins/Hill MacGibbon, 1985

Muddles
Mike Blantyres Software
Production Associates, 1986

Police — language in evidence
Cambridge Software House

Rates
City of Bath Technical College
ALBSU, 1985

Speedread
Arthur Rope
Wida Software, 1984

Textplay
Cambridge Micro Software
Cambridge University Press, 1986

The cloze program
N Young
AVP Computing, 1986

The Domesday project
devised jointly by Acorn, BBC and
Philips
Acorn Computers/BBC

Wordplay
Cambridge Micro Software
Cambridge University Press, 1986

Wordskill
Chalksoft

Wordstore
C Jones
Wida Software, 1985

Video

Another page
Kentucky Educational Television
1982

Finding things out
Audio Visual Products
ILEA, 1984

Options
COIC, 1985

Resources for tutors

Print

*A catalogue of resources for
teaching English as a second
language*
NATESLA National Extension
College, 1984

Adult literacy resources pack
ABE group
ALBSU, 1981

Adult numeracy training book
Scottish Community Education
Council

*An introduction to literacy
teaching*
ABE group ALBSU, 1980

*Basic education 16-99: a handbook
for tutors*
Martin Good, Rachel Jenkins,
Sheila Leevers and Andrew Pates
National Extension College, 1981

Each one strengthens each one
Avril Blay, Janis Novitzsky and
Julia Rosenak
Broadcasting Support Services,
1986

Extending reading skills
six ABE organisers
ALBSU, 1987

Helping adults to read
Tom MacFarlane
Macmillan, 1979

How's it going?: an alternative to testing students in adult literacy
Martin Good and John Holmes
ALBSU, 1982

How to find and adapt titles and select media
R Lewis and N Paine
CET, 1986

It used to be cheating: working together in literacy groups
Jane Lawrence
National Extension College, 1984

Literacy and numeracy materials: a guide
Cambridge Training and Development Ltd
Manpower Services Commission, 1988

Literacy work with bi-lingual students
Monica Turner
ALBSU, 1985

Making materials: a handbook for creative language teaching
Robert Leach
National Extension College, 1984

Making the most of tax forms
ALBSU, 1982

Moving ahead: a handbook for tutors of the mentally handicapped
Scottish Community Education Council

Resources: a guide to materials in adult literacy and basic skills
Cambridge Training and Development Ltd
ALBSU, 1986

Second chances: the national guide to adult education and training opportunities
Cambridge Training and Development Ltd
COIC, 1988

Send a friend a letter: workbook for students of letter writing
Scottish Community Education Council

Teaching literacy and numeracy to craft students
ALBSU, 1983

Tutoring in ABE: a training pack in 5 units, adult learning, planning a programme, reading, writing, working with groups
Scottish Community Education Council

Viewpoints 4: Literacy for what?
ABE tutors
ALBSU, 1985

Viewpoints 7
ABE practitioners
ALBSU, 1987

Women start here: a guide to setting up a women's group
Scottish Community Education Council

Words: a dictionary designed for work with hearing impaired adults
Scottish Community Education Council

Working together: an approach to functional literacy
nine practitioners ALBSU, 1987

Audio

Learning from experience
Jane Mace
Broadcasting Support Services, 1980

Video

Adult literacy – a publicity programme
ALBSU, 1983

Afro-Caribbean language issues: some student views
Afro Caribbean Language and Literacy Project
ILEA Learning Resources Branch, 1985

A mixed ability class in an adult education institute
ILEA TV Centre
ILEA, 1984

Barriers
Getting involved
Success story
Mersey Screen TV Productions
TV Video Productions, 1985

Helping with spelling
ALBSU, 1979

Teaching adults to read
ALRA ALBSU, 1977

SOURCES OF HELP

ACER
Wyvil School
Wyvil Road
London SW8
(01) 627 2662

Adult Literacy and Basic Skills Unit (ALBSU)
Kingsbourne House
229-231 High Holborn
London WC1V 7DA
(01) 405 4017
the major national body concerned with promoting adult literacy and basic education. It also has a database of resources which contains over 5000 items, published and unpublished, from major suppliers and from local schemes; publishes *Viewpoints* and *Adult Literacy and Basic Skills* newsletter

ABE Services
The Scottish Community Education Council
West Coates House
90 Haymarket Terrace
Edinburgh EH12 5LQ
National body for Scotland to promote and support the development of Adult Basic Education, offer training and materials for tutors and students

Advisory Centre for Education (ACE)
18 Victoria Park Square
London EC2 9PB
(01) 980 4596
publishes *ACE bulletin*

Avanti Books
1 Wellington Road
Stevenage
Herts SG2 9HR
(0438) 350155
major supplier of many resource
materials in adult basic education,
offering conference, display and
mail order services

BBC Publications
5 Marylebone High Street
London W1M 4AA
(01) 580 5577

*Cambridge Training and
Development Ltd*
43 Clifton Road
Cambridge CB1 4FB
(0223) 411464

Central Office of Information
Hercules Road
London SE1 7DU
(01) 486 8221

*Centre for Research into the
Education of Adults*
University of Nottingham
Cherry Tree Buildings
University Park
Nottingham NG7 2RD
(0602) 506101

Channel 4
Education Liaison Officer
Channel 4 TV
60 Charlotte Street
London W1P 2AX

Commission for Racial Equality
Elliot House
10-12 Allington Street
London SW1E 5EH
(01) 828 7022

*Department of Education and
Science*
Publications Despatch Centre
Honeypot Lane
Canons Park
Stanmore
Middlesex HA7 1AZ

*Department of Education and
Science*
Welsh Office Education
Department
Crown Building
Cathays Park
Cardiff CF1 3NQ
(0222) 825111

Further Education Unit
Elizabeth House
York Road
London SE1 7AH
(01) 934 9000

*Independent Broadcasting
Authority*
70 Brompton Road
London SW3 1EY
(01) 584 7011

*Local adult basic education or
community education*
contact your Local Education
Authority

Local Government Training Board
Arndale House
Arndale Centre
Luton LU1 2TS
(0582) 451166

4 BITS AND PIECES

MARIS-NET
Bank House
1 St Mary's Street
Ely
Cambs CB7 4ER
(0353) 61284
database of self-study materials,
organisations and services, *Open
learning bibliography, Trainer
support services, Adult training.*
Access to some services, and
information on subscription rates,
workshops etc available via Prestel
page *44560#

*National Association for Teaching
English as a Second Language to
Adults (NATESLA)*
Leith Adult Education Centre
4 Duncan Place
Edinburgh EH8 8JE
publishes a journal: *Language
issues*

*National Federation of Voluntary
Literacy Schemes*
Cambridge House
131 Camberwell Road
London SE5 OHF
(01) 703 8083

*National Institute of Adult
Continuing Education (NIACE)*
19b de Montfort Street
Leicester LE1 7GE
(0553) 551451
publishes several journals
including *Yearbook of adult
continuing education, Studies in
the education of adults,* and *Adult
education*

National Extension College
18 Brooklands Avenue
Cambridge CB2 2HN
(0223) 316644

*National Foundation for
Educational Research in England
and Wales*
The Mere
Upton Park
Slough
Berks SL1 2DQ
(0753) 74123

*National Federation of Voluntary
Literacy Schemes*
Cambridge House
131 Camberwell Road
London SE5 0HF
(01) 703 8083

*National Association for the Care
and Resettlement of Offenders
(NACRO)*
169 Clapham Road
London SW9 0PU
(01) 582 6500

National Interactive Video Centre
24-32 Stephenson Way
London NW1 2HD

Network
74 Victoria Crescent Road
Glasgow G12 9JN
Telephone referral service

*Northern Ireland Adult Literacy
Liaison Group*
c/o Department of Education
Rathgael House
Baloo Road
Bangor
Co Down BT19 2PR
(0274) 466311

*Northumberland College of Arts
and Technology*
College Road
Ashington
Northumberland NE63 6RG
(0670) 813248
special needs provision includes
a supported self-study materials
room

*Open University Continuing
Education Programme*
ASCO
PO Box 76
Milton Keynes MK7 6AN
(0908) 74066

Open College
101 Wigmore Street
London W1H 9AA
(01) 935 8088

The Open College in Scotland
Corunna House
29 Cadogan Street
Glasgow G2 7LP

*Research and Practice in Adult
Literacy (RAPAL)*
Department of Educational
Research
Lancaster University
Lancaster LA1 4YL
or
Bolton Royd Centre
Manningham Lane
Bradford
West Yorks BD8 7BB
(0274) 46812
exists to improve communication
between practitioners in adult
basic education by organising
conferences and workshops, and
also publishing a regular bulletin

Resource centres
local careers offices,
teachers'/curriculum development
centres, libraries and Citizens'
Advice Bureaux

*Scottish Centre for the Tuition of
the Disabled*
(Learning Links)
Queen Margaret's College
Clerwood Terrace
Edinburgh EM12 8TS

*Scottish Institute of Adult
Continuing Education*
30 Rutland Square
Edinburgh EH1 2BW

*Special Education Microelectronic
Resource Centres (SEMERCs)*
software for special needs may be
seen at SEMERCs — telephone
for details of open days

Bristol SEMERC
Bristol Polytechnic
Redland Hill
Bristol BS6 6UZ
(0272) 733141

Manchester SEMERC
Manchester Polytechnic
Elizabeth Gaskell Site
Hathersage Road
Manchester M13 OJA
(061) 225 9054

Newcastle SEMERC
Newcastle Polytechnic
Coach Lane Campus
Newcastle upon Tyne NE7 7XA
(091) 266 5057

Redbridge SEMERC
Dane Centre
Melbourne Road
Ilford
Essex
(01) 478 6363

*Special Educational Needs
Database (SEND)*
74 Victoria Crescent
Glasgow G12 9JN
public access database
containing information on
projects, SEMERCs etc; also
on Prestel page *SEND#

*Scottish Association for the Care
and Resettlement of Offenders*
SACRO
53 George Street
Edinburgh EH2 2ET

4 BITS AND PIECES

Training Access Points (TAPs)
The TAP Unit
Training Commission
St Mary's House
c/o Moorfoot
Sheffield S1 4PQ
(0742) 738611
databases giving information
about local education and training
opportunities as well as access to
NERIS, MARIS-NET and other
national databases; computer
terminals are situated in
jobcentres and some local
libraries

Training Commission
Moorfoot
Sheffield S1 4PQ
(0742) 753275

Video Arts Ltd
Dumbarton House
68 Oxford Street
London W1N 9LA
(01) 637 7288

Workers' Educational Association
Temple House
9 Upper Berkeley Street
London W1H 8BY
(01) 402 5608/9
organises various local classes
and also publishes *Workers'
Educational Association News*

*Workers' Educational Association
Scotland*
Riddle's Court
Edinburgh EH1 2PG

Workers' Educational Association
(NW)
2nd Floor
769 Stockport Road
Levenshulme
Manchester M19 3DL
(061) 224 7014

5 RESOURCES FOR
PHOTOCOPYING

Use these resources to support you when you are assessing learners' needs and when you are running group or individual sessions. All the resources are referred to in the text. They can be used directly or adapted to suit your circumstances.

For Assessment

Checklist Personal profile

For Sessions

Handout 1, Safety signs

Handout 2, One hundred key words

Handout 3, Everyday words

Handout 4, Dictionaries and directories

CHECKLIST

HOW'S YOUR READING?

	confident	not so confident	need help	no need
reading a newspaper or magazine				
books for yourself				
stories to children				
job adverts				
road signs				
timetables				
maps				
instructions				
cheques				
letters				
forms and leaflets				
invoices				
catalogues				
labels				
packets				
diagrams				
notes in handwriting				
dictionaries				
computer screens				
phone directories				
reference books				
structure words				
social words				
letter names and the alphabet				
word and letter shapes				
letter sounds and patterns				
syllables				
grammar				
punctuation and layout				
predicting (getting meaning from the context)				
reading between the lines				
skimming and scanning				
proofreading				
asking for help				
choosing reading materials				
anything else				

I would like to use reading to ....

....

....

The main reading I would like to work on ....

....

....

I would like to start with ....

....

....

My comments..

....

....

Name: ....

Date:..

PERSONAL PROFILE

Name:... Date:...

What I need to read	Purpose for reading	Knowledge	Skills

Safety signs

Look at these safety signs and match the words with each one.

NO SMOKING	**NO NAKED FLAME**
NO ENTRY	**FIRE HAZARD**
FIRE HOSE REEL	**NON DRINKING WATER**
FIRST AID BOX	**FIRE EXTINGUISHER**
DANGER ZONE	**NO PEDESTRIANS**

One hundred key words

Here are the 100 most common words in English.

The twelve most common

a   and   he   I   in   is   it
of   that   the   to   was

The twenty next most common

all   are   as   at   be   but   for
had   have   him   his   not   on   one
said   so   they   we   with   you

The sixty-eight next most common

about   an   back   been   before   big   by   call   came
can   come   could   did   do   down   first   from
get   go   has   her   here   if   into   just   like
little   look   made   make   me   more   much   must
my   new   no   now   off   old   only   or   other   our
out   over   right   see   she   some   their   them
then   there   this   two   up   want   well   went
were   what   when   where   which   who   will   your

Keep a lookout to see if you agree with this list. Make your own if you don't agree!

Everyday words

Here are some important words you see everywhere − in the street, at home, at work, in shops.

address

doctor

entrance

exit

ladies

gents

hospital

post office

queue here

staff only

enquiries

please

police

danger

signature

street

road

push

pull

wet paint

Look out for others you need. Make a note of them here.

Dictionaries and directories

The dictionary I find best to use is:

Its good points are:

To use a dictionary I need to know:

The alphabet forwards:

The alphabet backwards:

Other books of the same sort:

Points to remember about directories/catalogues etc:

COIC is one of the largest publishers of careers, occupational information and vocation-related training materials in the United Kingdom. Its fundamental aim is to produce accurate, unbiased and value-for-money products. Based in Sheffield, this unit is actively involved in research, development and production of all these materials. COIC products in the form of booklets, resource packs, games, videos and software are highly regarded by authoritative bodies, including schools, the careers service, tutors, managing agents and sponsors in training schemes.

Developed by Cambridge Training and Development Ltd, 43 Clifton Road, Cambridge CB1 4FB with Alison Wedgbury

Published by The Careers and Occupational Information Centre Moorfoot Sheffield S1 4PQ

Working on Reading was researched and written with the close co-operation of the Adult Literacy and Basic Skills Unit (ALBSU)

ISBN 0 86110 502 8

Further copies of this book and information about the wide range of materials produced by COIC, including details of prices, can be obtained by writing to:

COIC
Room W1103 Moorfoot Sheffield S1 4PQ

See COIC on Prestel ★ 270